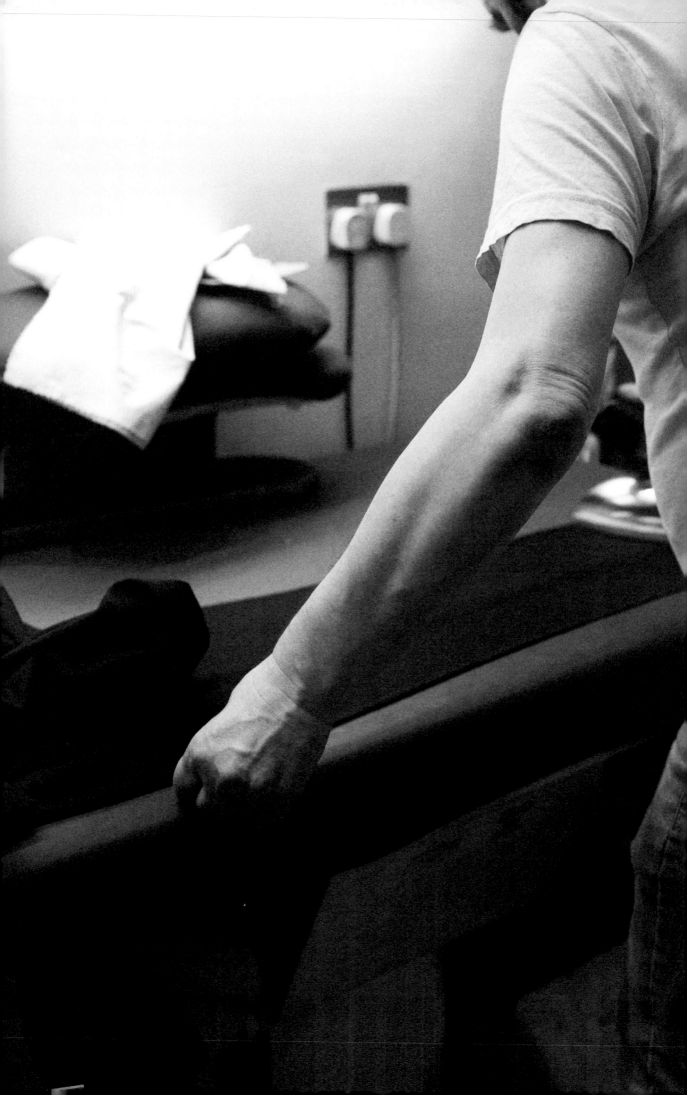

# MAKING THE CUT

## STORIES OF SARTORIAL ICONS BY SAVILE ROW'S MASTER TAILOR

with 230 illustrations

Richard Anderson

**Thames & Hudson**

# FOREWORD 18

by Dylan Jones

# INTRODUCTION 20

# A GOOD SHAPE: PATTERN- AND SUITMAKING BASICS 26

# LIGHT FARE 36

Single-Breasted Red Seersucker Coat with Double-Breasted Peaked Lapel 38
Single-Breasted Turquoise Crepe Coat 44
Single-Breasted Lilac Gabardine Asymmetric Coat 50
Single-Breasted Cream Linen Waistcoat 56
Mint-Green Cash-Cot Safari Coat 62
Double-Breasted Navy Blue Cashmere-Silk Dressing Gown 68

# STRONG SUITS 74

Single-Breasted Japanese Denim Suit 76
Double-Breasted Suit in Black Asymmetric Pinstripe 82
Single-Breasted Suit in 'Harvey Check' 88

# ATYPICAL TWEEDS 94

Single-Breasted Coat in Patchwork Tweed 96
Single-Breasted Three-Piece Suit in Italian Donegal Tweed 102
Two-Piece Shooting Suit with Pleated Back in Lovat Thornproof Tweed 108
Single-Breasted Coat in Ardalanish Pebble Diamond Twill 114

# TOP COATS 120

Classic Pea Coat in Orange Billiard-Table Baize 122
Red Melton Duffel Coat 128
Single-Breasted Orange Cord Raglan Car Coat 134
Classic Bomber Jacket in Irish Donegal Tweed 140
Double-Breasted Large Black-and-White Prince of Wales Check Overcoat 146
Single-Breasted Black Alpaca Dress Overcoat 152

# REGALIA REDUX 158

Single-Breasted Two-Button Frock Coat in Black Barathea 160
Tartan Morning Coat 166
Hunt Morning Coat in Scarlet Cashmere 172
Charcoal Nehru Coat with Polka-Dot Lining 178
Light Blue Single-Breasted Dinner Jacket in Wool Denim 184
Single-Breasted Black Sequined Dinner Jacket 190

Glossary 196
Acknowledgments 207
Picture Credits 207
About the Author 208

# FOREWORD

London is the home of menswear. We invented the suit, and in Savile Row we have the most important men's shopping street in the world. While the Row has always appealed to the establishment, in the last two decades it has opened itself up so much that it now attracts customers of all tastes and from all corners, seeking the best in everything from traditional suiting to contemporary formal wear. Just look at Richard Anderson, who has been a pillar of the Row since he and Brian Lishak opened their doors at No. 13 Savile Row in 2001. Together with their team of expert tailors, they pride themselves not only on their many innovations, but also on the perfect fit and exceptional quality of service they offer their customers. To maintain the heritage of Savile Row while offering innovative, forward-looking design is not an easy balance to strike, but at Richard Anderson they do so beautifully. The stories and garments showcased in this book celebrate the care, skill and imagination Richard and his colleagues bring to every piece they make, whether bespoke or ready-to-wear.

Richard Anderson is part of the new breed of tailors who have taken not just London, but also the world by storm, by catering to a new kind of customer who isn't only interested in pinstripes and brogues. This new boom in British menswear is something I tried to reflect when, at the behest of the British Fashion Council, I helped to set up London's first men's fashion week, London Collections Men (or London Fashion Week Men's, as it's now called) at the end of 2011. Although the idea of a fashion week dedicated especially to men started from the desire to compete on the global stage with the likes of Paris, Milan and New York – the other major cities that have held similar weeks for years – it was crucial to us to include Savile Row in our week, so that London reflected not just the big British brands and emerging designers, and not just the international megabrands who wanted to use London as a hub. For this reason it was an honour to be able to host the independent Savile Row tailors, and especially an honour to host Richard Anderson and his colleagues.

Long may they thrive!

Dylan Jones

# INTRODUCTION

A man cannot make love with any kind of conviction unless
he is wearing a coat cut within half a mile of Piccadilly.
  – *The Tailor and Cutter* trade journal, *c.* 1860

etting aside for a moment the merits of wearing a coat while making love: more than 150 years later it remains indisputable that the world's finest suits still hail from London's Savile Row. Couturiers elsewhere have progressed admirably, but when it comes to custom-made clothing there is simply no substitute for nearly three centuries of sartorial and, indeed, psychological experience – the privileged inheritance of a tailor trained on the Row or in its immediate vicinity, classic tailoring's 'Golden Mile'. Savile Row's dedicated patronage by the world's most celebrated entertainers, athletes, businessmen, politicians and royalty attests to its corner on the very personification of eminence, a tradition uniting kings of England and dukes of York with Napoleon, Charles Dickens, Benjamin Disraeli, JFK, Cary Grant, Bing Crosby, Fred Astaire, Twiggy, Mick Jagger, Barbra Streisand, David Beckham, Sir Ian McKellen, Gianni Agnelli and Simon Cowell. Contrary to yesteryear, when a man's pedigree and references dictated whether or not a Savile Row tailor would even deign to measure his chest, these days anyone who can afford a Savile Row suit may buy one. As a result, more and more people are discovering first-hand that this seeming extravagance actually has a good deal of practical appeal: not one of the ten off-the-peg suits you could buy for the cost of a single bespoke one from Savile Row will fit nearly as well, look nearly as good, nor last nearly as long as the latter – in some cases, for life.

Thirty-five years ago, when I was seventeen, my father all but dragged me by the ear to an interview at Savile Row's Huntsman & Sons – at the time the world's most expensive and arguably most respected tailoring house. The vacancy was for an apprentice cutter, and, somewhat improbably, I was offered a three-month trial period, a gruelling audition that thanks to nerves and inexperience I very nearly failed. But pride prevailed and I dug in my heels for a further seventeen years of tailoring training unparalleled in perfectionism and prestige. Consequently, I became, at thirty-four, the youngest master cutter in Huntsman's 150-year history.

The terms cutter and tailor are often treated interchangeably, but there is a distinction, and it is a critical one. Technically speaking, the person who measures you and cuts your pattern is not actually a tailor, but a cutter. A tailor is someone who assembles the parts of a garment. A master cutter is the sartorial genie, if you will – the person who sizes you up in order to conceive and cut a unique paper pattern from which the ultimate suit will be made. According to the 1804 *Dictionary of English Trades*, his job, in part, is to 'bestow a good shape where nature has not granted one'. To this effect, the sizing-up process often requires a characterological as well as physical evaluation, for even a customer's temperament and sense of humour can go some way to dictating the lines of his ideal suit. His cutter would be doing only half the job if he were to rely on tape measurements alone.

When I started at Huntsman, its dedication to quality and, indeed, its expensiveness made it tailoring's standard-bearer. The clientele was society's crème de la crème, a cast of luminaries that included Gianni Agnelli,

Katharine Hepburn, Dirk Bogarde, J. J. Cartier, Douglas Fairbanks Jr, Gregory Peck, Bill Blass, Laurence Olivier, Peter Sellers, Bing Crosby, Paul Newman and Rex Harrison. For the majority, money was no object, and in any case the price was immaterial – factors crucial to the sustainability of Huntsman's superior work ethic, which was to achieve perfection at any cost. Most of Huntsman's clients had already auditioned every other tailoring house on the Row, and precisely because Huntsman was not only the best but also the priciest, its clients became loyal, knowing they could not demand better elsewhere. Of course, high price tags breed high maintenance, and some customers demanded near-miracles. These were people who tended to be at the top of their game, whether that of business, entertainment, seduction or sport – nothing less than flawless togs would do. And only on Savile Row, which Huntsman led in quality and cachet, could their pursuit of perfection be so indulgently accommodated.

Tragically, in the 1990s, Huntsman's prolonged heyday gave way to a period of decline. Retirement claimed its elder masters – my venerable mentors, Colin Hammick and Brian Hall – and the company was bought by a team of outside investors less interested in preserving quality than in slashing costs to manipulate revenue. That this might be the beginning of a Piccadilly-wide trend was a heartbreaking prospect: the emphasis on 'output' and 'cost-effectiveness', after all, is utterly antithetical to all that Savile Row stands for. Certainly at Huntsman it was the end of an era, and among those of us loyal to the old way of doing things this calamitous takeover inspired a collective crisis of conscience. Perfecting one's craft at any effort and expense is a principle unsustainable at a company whose standards had been so egregiously compromised for the sake of easy profit. And so I decided to resign from Huntsman, and – with a wife and four children to support – opened up my own shop, Richard Anderson Ltd, two doors down at No. 13. Luckily for me I was doing this with the invaluable help and wisdom of another Hunstman alum, Brian Lishak, who in 2016 celebrated his sixtieth anniversary of working on Savile Row.

Fifteen years later, a somewhat paradoxical reputation as Savile Row mavericks who struck out on our own in the name of tradition has won us the custom of many former Huntsman patrons as well as that of a new generation. Moreover, the arrival on the Row of non-bespoke haute couture houses such as Richard James and Ozwald Boateng has inspired among the other bespoke firms, as well, an increased experimentation with new fabrics, new colours and modern tastes. Far from a relic of yesteryear, Savile Row is a driver of modernity: in any trade or craft, it is precisely the technique and skills that have been passed down from generation to generation that give us the freedom to be creative in producing optimal results today. There is no reason – none I see, anyway – that this beloved British institution should not continuously embrace and update its traditions for real people, real bodies and modern times.

It is largely in this spirit that I have compiled this book, at once a compendium of classic tailoring's quintessential designs and a celebration of those garments' adaptability to the tastes and imagination of today. From the safari jacket to the pea coat, from Japanese denim to Hebridean wool, from black sequins to red seersucker, orange baize, green cashmere or patchwork tweed, what you see here is as much of the sartorial kaleidoscope we could possibly squeeze between two covers. In addition to offering up a bit of historical context for each piece, we describe how it is made – including, in many cases, any necessary concessions to the idiosyncrasies of working with a particular fabric – as well as providing vivid photos and original illustrations curated to inform, entertain and inspire. After all, there are two artists behind every article of bespoke clothing conceived on Savile Row: the cutter and the customer. It is the customer who chooses the fabric, the style, the embellishments or, indeed, the understated simplicity that makes the commission his own. So, to all you aspiring designers out there, whether fashion is your livelihood or your leisure, this book – our bible of sartorial heritage, craft and creativity – is for you.

*Overleaf: Figuration photographs of tailoring clients taken by cutters in the early 1970s.*

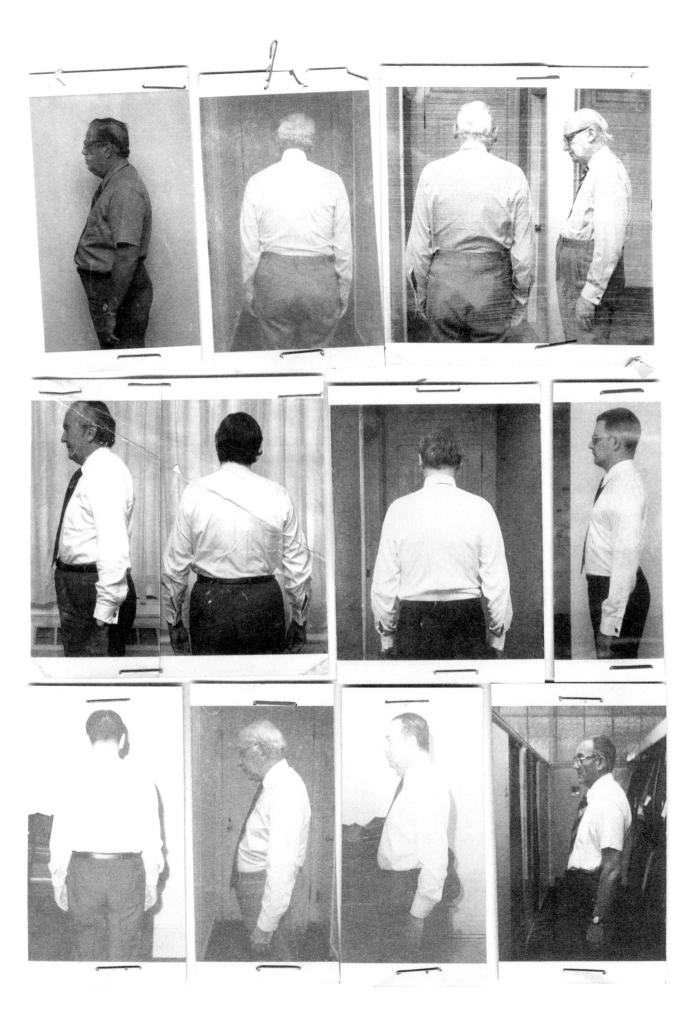

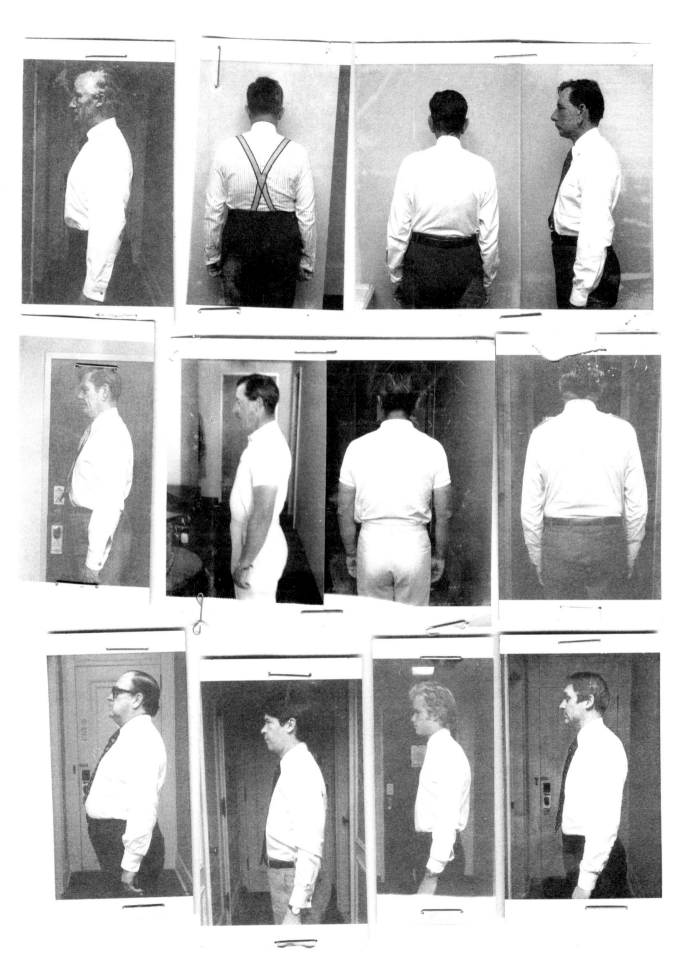

# A GOOD SHAPE: PATTERN- AND SUITMAKING BASICS

**L**ike the garment itself, the method by which a bespoke piece is made is different every time. Even if two customers have the exact same measurements and choose the exact same material – even if they want the exact same style coat, waistcoat, dressing gown or suit – there will still be idiosyncratic differences in carriage and stance, not to mention the inherent singularity of any artisanal process. Still, what follows is a general overview of what a customer can expect when he commissions an article of clothing on Savile Row.

### Choosing a cloth

Every new order for a bespoke garment begins with the customer choosing his cloth. In fact this is the origin of the term 'bespoke': the customer was understood to have 'spoken for' his fabric.

Several factors go into cloth selection. If a customer does not come in already strongly inclined (or, as once was customary and occasionally happens still, with an already selected and purchased piece of cloth in hand), his cutter will make a series of queries about the garment in question. When and where will it be worn? London in summer? New York in winter? A March wedding in the Caribbean? Is it only for a small handful of special occasions, or for more frequent wear? Often a cutter will advise a first-time client to start with a cloth that has a bit of weight to it, such as a medium-weight wool. This is so that the first garment made according to the customer's pattern will most accurately and enduringly hold the desired silhouette. If a customer seems inclined to choose a fabric his cutter thinks will prove a bad match for his purpose or visage, the cutter and sales person will speak up. Large checks, wide pinstripes and bright colours, for example, do not suit every frame. Certain complexions look better in a bold blue rather than a light grey, and vice versa. But at the end of the day it is the customer's suit and, whatever his preferences, his cutter will oblige.

Now, on to lining. Some houses on Savile Row have a 'signature lining' – a sort of calling card by which they are recognized. When I worked at Huntsman from 1982 to 2000, for example, this was a white silk with purple stripes of varying widths. We used it to line coatsleeves and waistbands, whereas the rest of a suit would be lined with silk or Ermazine chosen on an individual basis. It became common among bespoke tailors to use a different lining in the sleeves because clothes in earlier times were necessarily very heavy. There was no central heating, of course, and a good majority of bespoke tailoring's clientele lived in draughty homes and castles. The cloth and body linings they would select for their suits were heavy, perspiration-absorbent materials – namely alpaca, which was popular until shortly after the Second World War. But a heavy lining limited arm mobility, so many houses used a specially commissioned lighter lining in sleeves – and occasionally in pockets and trouser waistbands as well; indeed, wherever a 'thermal' lining was unnecessary – while the signature embellishments made for a smart touch. Today, of course, between global warming and advanced thermostat technology, staying warm is less of a concern, leaving customers to choose whichever lining they would like, along with other trimmings, from buttons to stitching or leather jettings on their pockets.

**Measuring the customer**

After discussing with the client his specific aesthetic desires, the master cutter ushers the customer into a fitting room and proceeds to take the necessary measurements. Each house and perhaps even each cutter within a house has a preferred method for measurement-taking; in my case, if the garment in question is a standard two-piece lounge suit, there will be, on average, nineteen measurements in all.

First, the fourteen measurements for the coat. As he holds his tape measure this way and that, the master cutter calls out each measurement while his apprentice, standing off to the side, repeats them back to him and jots the numbers down. The first seven measurements are taken while the customer is wearing a coat – his own coat or one of our model coats in his approximate size. Then the remaining seven measurements are taken with the coat off. The final product is an amalgamation of these two sets of figures.

For example:

'Natural waist seventeen and one-quarter,' I might call out. This is the distance from the customer's neck down to the small of his back.

'Seventeen and one-quarter,' my apprentice would echo, writing it down.

'Coat length thirty-one and one-quarter.'

'Thirty-one and one-quarter.'

'Half cross back eight and a quarter.'

'Eight and a quarter.'

'Centre seam to elbow twenty-one and one-quarter ... Centre seam to cuff thirty-two ... Front button to side seam thirteen and a half ... Side seam to centre back twenty and three-eighths ...'

Encouraging a customer to stand naturally can sometimes be tricky, but it is essential to a successful process, since you want to assess the client's posture in the most characteristic position possible. If we sense a client standing 'over-erectly', we will gently encourage him to relax. Failing that, we will note down the unnatural posture and adjust our measurements accordingly.

Now, with the customer in his shirtsleeves:

'Scye depth back nine and three-quarters.' This is the distance from the collar stud position at the nape of neck to the centre-back position in parallel with the base of the left scye, confirmed by the placing of a metal square with a tape measure. (A contraction of the words 'arm's' and 'eye', scye is the round opening in a coat into which a sleeve is inserted.)

'Nine and three-quarters!'

'Front shoulder fifteen and a half.'

'Fifteen and a half!'

'Over shoulder twenty-two and one-quarter ... Chest thirty-nine ...

Coat waist thirty-three and a half … Coat seat forty and a quarter …
Scye to centre front eight and a quarter.'

'Eight and a quarter!'

When the coat measurements have been collected, it is then time to measure the customer five times over in his trousers: outside seam, inside seam, waist, seat and width of bottoms. Throughout the measuring process, the cutter is also making mental notes as to the customer's figuration – his natural carriage and anatomical particularities, from the subtle to the severe. Is one shoulder higher than the other? (99% of us are slightly lower on the right.) Do they slope or are they square? Is one hip more prominent? Is his back rounded or flat? How does he walk? Confidently, with his shoulders back, or tipped forward a little, with a slump? Not that you ask these questions aloud, mind you; it's more a matter of deducing the answers from what you observe. Accordingly, this subjective component to the measuring process is perhaps the most esoteric part of conceiving a pattern from scratch: qualitative rather than quantitative, it is a form of assessment that verges on the psychological.

**Creating the pattern**

Measurements and figuration notes in hand, the cutter then constructs and cuts a paper pattern consisting of five templates. These are: three for the jacket (a back, forepart and sleeve) and two for the trousers (a topside, for the front of the leg, and an underside, for the back). This pattern should not only accommodate the customer's dimensions but also flatter his overall figure and complement his individual style.

The ability to visualize a body even when its owner is no longer standing right in front of you – to convert his two-dimensional pattern into a three-dimensional image in your mind – is called Rock of Eye. A reliable mind's eye puts a cutter one step ahead of the game, for it allows him to envision how the body in question will interact with its pattern even before the customer returns for his next fitting. Of course, it does not hurt to get started on your pattern as soon as possible after sizing up your customer, if your schedule and workload will allow.

Like my Huntsman mentors before me, I use the antiquated Thornton System, immortalized in a book published in 1893 entitled *The Sectional System of Gentlemen's Garment Cutting (comprising coats, vests, breeches, and trousers, &c.)* by J. P. Thornton. Editor of the *Minister's Gazette of Fashion* and founder of the London Alliance of West End Cutters, Thornton was as much a philosopher as a practitioner of his trade. Accordingly, *The Sectional System* reads in places as something like a Sartrean proof:

The difficulties of trouser cutting may be concisely summed up as follows:
If a trouser is cut to fit a man whose legs and body are in a straight position, thus:
How can it fit the same individual when his legs and body are in a crooked position? thus:

How can the two cloth cylinders, suitable for the straight legs, fit without forming folds in the laps and under the knees when the wearer is seated? thus:

I will myself supply the answer and say, in no possible way can it be done, and yet this is the demand that the tailor time after time is called upon to meet ... But it must not be assumed that because absolute perfection, or impossibility, is not attainable, that we can afford to disregard the problems presented, and depend for our success in trouser cutting (for mankind will still wear them and tailors must still make them) upon the mercy of our customers. This would be a policy that only need be mentioned to be condemned. No trousers are in all positions perfect, but it is almost unnecessary to add that some are greatly superior to the majority, while just a few in their adaptable fitting qualities and general style or 'hang' are worthy of the trade and a credit to those constituting it.

Thus:

To cut a piece of clothing according to the Thornton System is not merely to follow a series of objective instructional diagrams, but also to appeal to a kind of philosophical calling that prizes the pursuit of perfection. One begins by taking up one's square, tailoring scale and freshly sharpened chalk, and drawing what one envisions as the coat's shoulder-line and spine: a massive T.

Then you mark your crucial reference points, which are the natural waist measurement, 17¼ inches, and the coat length, which is 3¼. Now mark your depth of scye, which is 9¾, and square across all three. At the waist point, come in 1⅜ and from here square down from the neck point; this is your centre back. Come in ⅜ at your natural waist to ¼ at bottom and again square down to achieve your run into the small of the back. Note your half cross back measurement, which is 8¼, and halve your depth of scye and from 4⅞ draw your half cross back line from the back's midpoint to the scye and square up.

Now look to the bottom of the coat and visualize where the customer's hip point should be. Mark it. Halve the coat-off seat measurement, which is 40¼, and mark this point on your thirds scale, plus ½ inch. Now angle the line slightly into the waist, and with your square connect the length of the coat to the waist. Mark your over shoulder, which is 22¼, adding 1 inch. Then, using your eighth, quarter and half scales, mark three points and connect them with a crescent – this is your armhole. Then shape the neck. Halve your chest measure, which is 39, so mark 19½ plus an extra ⅛ on the sixth scale. Square up and also come up 1 inch for the collar, then round it out to connect to the shoulder point. Now add some shape to the sides: bring it in a little at the waistline and out around the seat, so it kicks out a bit at the hips. At which point, you've completed the back.

Now, using your weights balanced on your square, spread what you've done over a fresh piece of paper for reference in making the forepart.

Halve your chest measurement, which gives you 19½, then take that measure from the centre back and mark 2 inches and another 2 inches. Mark the quarter chest again from the centre back, 9¾, plus the addition of 3½ as a standard measure. From the 3½ point to the first 2-inch point, halve and square up for the front shoulder. Then, at the 3½ point, square up for the over shoulder. Square up and down from the farthest 2-inch point to gain your front-edge run. Use the back to gain the side seam run, and then insert a pencil tip through the reinforced hole at the end of your measuring tape and hold its fulcrum at the pattern's neckpoint while swinging your makeshift pendulum across the paper's surface. This gives you the coat's convex bottom edge. With a similar gesture, you create its waist. Then you sketch in one or two buttons, the deep curve of the neck and lapel, the armhole and one or more darts, and, finally, a sleeve – each step bringing you closer to completing a balanced pattern that resembles a garment in 'real life'.

In short: the process is a scaled algorithm combined with a bit of join-the-dots. But then, as we've said, the quantitative part is only half the job. One's figuration notes, Rock of Eye and even a character assessment of your wearer must then also be summoned to transform the draft pattern into one that will 'bestow a good shape where nature has not granted one'. Indeed, because they influence posture, carriage and one's personal style, even a customer's temperament and sense of humour can go some way toward dictating the lines of his ideal suit. So now one must consider as well how to accommodate, say, a 'corpulent figure'. And yet, because not every shape that walks in the door is exactly like the last one, there is unsettlingly little objectivity in exactly how best to elongate a man's trunk and boost his backside, never mind that we have not yet accounted for his relative jocularity. Does he stoop? Are his arms of dissimilar length, or does he have uneven shoulder blades, which will affect how the garment hangs? To counter a hunched back, one generally cuts a coat pattern shorter than average in the front, longer than average in the back, and smaller and tighter around the neck, in order to keep the balanced back and foreparts in place. An off-the-peg – or even badly made bespoke – coat breaks down in three areas on a hunched body: the back of the coat strains on top and collapses below, its collar bunches up, and the front hangs long and loose from the body. But in a bespoke coat not only made according to careful measurements but also with practised figuration and Rock of Eye, once one area is adjusted, the others start to fall into place.

If a customer who has already had a pattern made comes back for a new garment, we run a tape around his every relevant dimension again, to check whether any shrinkage or expansion has occurred. If so, the existing pattern is amended. When I am finally satisfied with a new or amended pattern, I indicate the requested style features on the order's paper ticket, which in the case of a two-piece suit would specify the following: the catalogue number and weight of the selected cloth; whether the coat is to be single- or double-breasted; how many buttons; how many pockets (inbreast, outbreast, or ticket right- or left-cross); how many vents; whether the trousers should be straight-top or scalloped for braces; whether they should have straight or slanted side pockets and an extra pocket for keyfobs; whether they should have pleats or plain legs; turn-ups or straight hems – and so on. The permutations with which the client may assert his personal sartorial requirements and style come to seem infinite.

Incidentally, cutting pattern paper is a completely different game from cutting cloth. Each cutter has his different shears for cutting paper and for cutting cloth – the paper shears are much smaller, their blades approximately 7 inches long, whereas cloth blades are 10. And while you might well ask what could be simpler than cutting paper, fashioning a highly accurate pattern with 7-inch shears is not as easy as it might seem.

### Striking the fabric

Once a paper pattern has been established and used to determine the amount of material that must be ordered, and the chosen fabric has then arrived, the pattern is meticulously arranged in a 'lay' on the material and its perimeter marked out with a piece of chalk shaped like a large guitar pick. This must be done not only accurately but also in the most economical way, so as to waste as little fabric as possible. One also must take into account the pattern of the fabric, if any: if you're using a checked material, such as a Prince of Wales check, you must add a bit of extra material on the length to allow for matching the squares or lines up at the edges. Moreover, one-way cloths must be cut with all parts of the pattern facing the same way, to avoid shading. Lightweight fabrics such as linens, cottons and silks also must be cut in the same direction, but with an extra allowance for shrinkage. The 'striker' – myself or an apprentice – then strikes, or cuts, the fabric around the pattern. More often than not these pieces are then handed over to the house basters, who assemble them with long, loose, easily removable white stitches for the first fitting. If a longtime customer's pattern has been established and is certain to be current and correct, the cut fabric is instead turned over directly to the shop's tailors for a more advanced assembly.

### Assembling the suit

To keep track of where each garment is in the making-up process, I use an old-fashioned card system that I inherited from my Huntsman mentors. I have used it for the last 25 years, and I remain convinced that it is superior to any customized software money that could buy. How does it work? Each customer is appointed his own little pink cutter card, to be filed alphabetically. Here the order's details are written: a unique job number, a description of the garment (for example, 'single-breasted navy mohair coat'), followed by a row of boxes indicating the different stages of make the garment would go through, and by whose hands.

A tick under 'alt' or 'tickets' means the customer has met with the company's credit criteria, signalling that the making of the garment may commence.

A tick under 'in cut' means that a paper pattern has been created by the master cutter and laid out on cloth by his striker, who has physically cut the cloth pieces, now ready for provisional assembly.

The initials under 'baster' identify which of my company's basters is responsible for the basting phase. No pockets or linings are put in at the basting stage; the idea is simply to create an accurate 'draft' of the paper pattern in cloth form. What basting does require is establishing a balanced relationship between the coat's back and foreparts while also accounting, at least preliminarily, for figuration: the master cutter's notes on the customer's posture, say, or on the aforementioned ill-matched shoulder blades. A mock collar made of canvas is shaped around the neck and more canvas inserted in the chest to give the coat some body. A new customer would typically undergo one, occasionally two, and in rare cases three fittings at this provisional stage, so that we can finalize the standard pattern before moving on to the more advanced tailoring, when alterations are likely to be more costly and time-consuming.

When both customer and cutter are happy with the baste and ready to proceed, one of my undercutters rips it down, that is, disassembles the coat using a penknife or bodkin, being extremely careful not to damage the material. Then the material is smoothed out for the next phase. The paper pattern is revised as necessary and again placed on the chosen cloth for any re-marking and re-cutting. The resulting pieces are then passed to one of my ten to twelve coatmakers, in the case of a coat, or to one of my eight to ten trousermakers, in the case of trousers. Included along with the basic pieces at this stage are all the trimmings: Ermazine, silesia or silk lining; collar canvas and melton; tropical syddo, white felt, horsehair and lapthair canvases for the front body panels; hand silk for fine stitching; buttons (or some other kind of fastener, such as silk knots or toggles) and buttonhole twist. The adjusted paper pattern is also included, for the tailors' reference.

An important component of this advanced assembly stage is padding. To pad a coat collar one uses what's called an undercollar, which typically measures 5 by 22 inches and is cut on the bias at an angle of 33 degrees. Undercollar canvas is wool with light pores throughout, strong yet flexible enough to respond to an iron. On top of the canvas undercollar you then baste in another undercollar of melton, a soft fabric in a colour matching the jacket it will eventually adorn. The melton undercollar is what is visible when you lift the collar at the nape and look at its underside. Regimented rows of tiny angled stitches give the collar canvas a slight curl, so that once connected to the coat it lies naturally around the neck. The insertion of materials into the chest to give it shape also demand extreme care and attention. Typically this is a length of wool syddo, which is heavy or light depending on the weight of fabric to be used for the coat itself. Also inserted in the chest are a piece of white felt and a piece of natural horsehair canvas. The syddo spends a night in a sink to shrink, and is then left to dry before being pressed. The forepart pattern is then placed on the canvas and each side cut. The canvas runs the length of the coat, filling the whole shoulder before angling down through the chest and finishing just inside the front dart. On the forepart a puff cut is taken to the top of the canvas at the shoulder's midpoint and cut to approximately 5 inches down. This helps to prevent the shoulder from stringing, that is, acquiring a corrugated appearance, later in the coat's life.

At this point the horsehair is basted to the chest and the white felt placed on top. Now a dozen or so intricate rows of hand stitches attach the three types of canvas together and a 14-pound iron is applied to the layers to finish a light but pliable chest area that over time will mould to the body underneath.

From the baste through this 'forward phase' generally takes two to three weeks. Then the coat is returned to the master cutter now looking much more like the finished article. The shoulders and facings have been finished by hand; the side seams and pockets machined in securely; and the hand-padded body canvas and handmade shoulder pads have been inserted. But there is still no top collar or finished buttonholes, and the sleeve and body linings are only basted into place. A tick under 'fwd' indicates that this phase is now complete.

When the forward fitting has taken place, the garment is then returned to its respective tailors for any remaining adjustments and finishing. Changes at this point are expected to be minimal: raising the collar ever so slightly, wadding in the shoulders a bit more, lengthening or shortening the sleeves, taking in or letting out the side seams. When these alterations have been made, the garment is turned over to fine-fingered tailoresses who 'fell', or stitch, the delicate lining to the coat and perform other detailed hand work such as lining the pockets and stitching buttonholes. Then the suit is pressed, a highly specialized and underrated stage in itself since a bad press can go some way to undoing all of the work done up to this point. Finally, the buttons are sewn on.

Trousers, by contrast, tend to undergo only a single baste; then they are fitted on the customer, finished, and fitted once more. Alterations range from the more minor tweaks to letting out the waist, seat and fork, as well as lengthening the legs by feathering (tearing) a piece of paper and carefully gluing it as an extension onto the existing pattern to achieve the correct measure. Similarly, when a customer has lost weight, or requires some other adjustment, we change the pattern at each such stage to accord with the new measurements or request. If the customer gains back the weight, the trimmed patterns be 'let out' again with more feathered extensions and a glue stick.

When all of this has been done, a tick can at last be made under 'FIN'.

*Sketch showing the basic measures to be taken for a coat.*

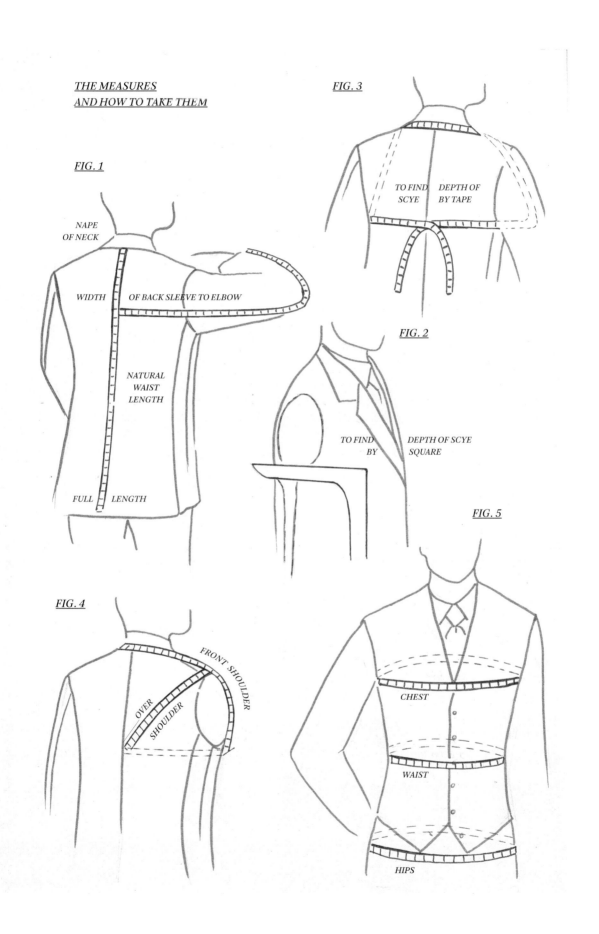

THE MEASURES
AND HOW TO TAKE THEM

FIG. 3

FIG. 1

TO FIND    DEPTH OF
SCYE       BY TAPE

NAPE
OF NECK

WIDTH    OF BACK SLEEVE TO ELBOW

FIG. 2

NATURAL
WAIST
LENGTH

TO FIND    DEPTH OF SCYE
BY         SQUARE

FULL    LENGTH

FIG. 5

FIG. 4

FRONT SHOULDER

OVER

SHOULDER

CHEST

WAIST

HIPS

# LIGHT FARE

SINGLE-
BREASTED
RED
SEERSUCKER
COAT WITH
DOUBLE-
BREASTED
PEAKED LAPEL

The word *seersucker* derives from the Persian words for 'milk' (*shir*) and 'sugar' (*shakar*), allegedly because the smoothness of milk and the granularity of sugar bear some resemblance to the material's alternating textures. This duality is achieved by what is called a slack-tension weave, whereby threads are wound onto two warp beams such that the fibers bunch up, giving seersucker its corrugated look. This process is also responsible for the material's somewhat stiff quality, which causes it to stand slightly apart from the wearer's body, dissipating heat and circulating air. For this reason seersucker evokes images of British colonialists and gentlemen sipping lemonade in the American South; it's one of the most comfortable fabrics to wear in the world's sultriest locations, from Bombay to Baton Rouge.

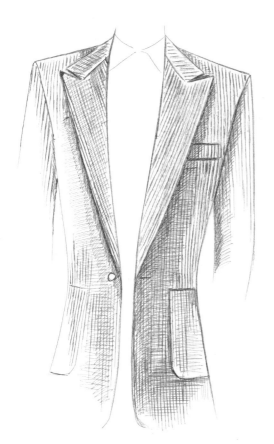

A cousin of seersucker is also associated with the American Old West, where, once upon a time, a heavier, navy-and-white-striped fabric called 'hickory stripe' was the most popular choice for making up the overalls, jackets and caps worn by railroad engineers. (Dickies, a work-clothes manufacturer founded a century ago in Texas, still makes durable and affordable hickory stripe items with charmingly practical details such as 'pencil divisions' and 'hammer loops'.) In the 1920s, the American writer Damon Runyon took to wearing seersucker, a gesture the *New York Times* would later diagnose as 'reverse snobbery', given that at the time the fabric was typically the garb of oilyard toilers. ('[It is] causing much confusion among my friends,' said Runyon. 'They cannot decide whether I am broke or just setting a new vogue.') During the Second World War seersucker was used for the dress uniforms of the first female US Marine Corps reservists, not in the traditional blue-and-white version, but in a pistachio-green stripe, which from a distance has a solid seafoam appearance.

Today, true seersucker tends to be regarded as a highbrow but also casual affair, with a certain dash of debonair. Its reputation is owed in no small part to Gregory Peck having worn a blue-and-white three-piece suit as Atticus Finch in the film adaptation of *To Kill A Mockingbird* (1962). And even today a tradition started in 1996 by the American Senator Trent Lott, wanting to 'bring a little Southern charm to the Capitol', has ensured that a good number of the country's congressmen (and women) turn out for 'Seersucker Thursday', in a nod to how their predecessors would have

*Original working fashion sketch showing one-button red-and-white seersucker jacket with two patch pockets and peaked lapel.*

dressed before the blessing of air conditioning. Indeed, climate has a say in just about every notable fashion trend, and certainly was a reason that seersucker never achieved the status of a Huntsman staple. Accustomed as they were to working with heavier materials – as I've said, because heavier materials made for a crisper silhouette and were what had kept mid-twentieth-century Englishmen warm – my Huntsman mentors Colin Hammick and Brian Hall routinely declined to make suits in seersucker. Its inherent creasing, maintained Hammick, 'doesn't show off our line'. He and Hall would even suggest that the customer try Caraceni, an Italian suitmaker based in Rome, as though only a tailor plying his trade at near-

tropical latitude would have any reason to work with material so ethereal.

By the 1990s, however, cotton and seersucker suits had become much more common. This was thanks in part to central heating, with temperatures climbing outdoors as well – so much so that Brian Lishak and I dared to break ranks and organized Huntsman's first-ever seersucker promotion, which prompted many longtime Huntsman customers to come in, take one look at the estival model in the foyer and say: 'Oh. I didn't you know did this sort of thing,' – and then order one up directly. At Huntsman, we adhered more or less to the traditional American style, which is still wildly popular today: light blue and white, single-breasted, with three buttons down the front, one vent in the back. All that's missing is a gin and tonic. Then, when Richard Anderson Ltd was born, we made a slightly more rakish model, with patch pockets – i.e., pockets made of a separate piece of cloth, sewn to the outside of the coat – for a more youthful look. We also branched out into the model you see here: a bold red-and-white-striped jacket, single-breasted but with a double-breasted peaked lapel, which juxtaposes a bit of formality with the fabric's casual nature. To emphasize the contrast even further, we cut the lapel about an inch wider than usual: 4½ inches instead of 3½.

In the red-and-white stripe, we have so far made only jackets. Blue-and-white seersucker is a classic suit fabric but the red lends itself more to a coat worn on its own with khakis or jeans. We've made several of these, perfect for summer cocktail parties in Sag Harbor or the like. We've also made a tartan version, a relatively subdued grey-on-grey variation, and – unsurprisingly – dozens and dozens of coats, suits and trousers in good old blue-and-

*Above: The bold double-breasted peaked lapel with a 1-inch handmade lapel hole adds a touch of formality. Opposite: Gregory Peck wearing the quintessential three-piece seersucker suit as Atticus Finch in* To Kill A Mockingbird *(1962).*

white, including a fantastic double-breasted model for our good friend and former *Vogue* editor-at-large André Leon Talley. The blue-and-white fabric also features widely in our ready-to-wear range. After all, seersucker takes 'ready-to-wear' to a new level: not only is a seersucker suit ready to don off the rack, it is also ready to be worn after you've sat in it for hours on a plane, stuffed it into a locker, or – if you're so inclined – rolled it into a ball. Authentic seersucker will always spring back and look great. These days, weaving the real article is a slow process, which means there are a lot of cheaper, synthetic imitations. Often in such cases the puckering effect is achieved chemically and the fabric doesn't breathe as well as the natural original. Synthetic seersucker also tends to lose its shape over time – which, of course, is contrary to the point. The point of seersucker is to be cool and comfortable while also looking sharp. Even when all you're doing is sitting on the beach.

*Left: The red-and-white seersucker jacket exudes elegant informality, especially paired with jeans or khakis, perfect for a summer cocktail party outdoors.*

*Opposite: The distinctive puckered texture of seersucker keeps the fabric away from the wearer's skin, allowing air to circulate.*

# SINGLE-BREASTED TURQUOISE CREPE COAT

A popular fabric made of natural or synthetic fibres twisted and treated to give the material's surface a crinkled texture, crepe has come a long way from Victorian and Edwardian times, when it was associated primarily with widows' mourning clothes, generally referred to as *crape*. In the nineteenth and early twentieth centuries, whenever they went out of doors, widowed British women were expected to wear a black crepe-trimmed dress and veiled bonnet – a fashion adhered to so devoutly that Courtaulds, a UK-based fabric and chemical manufacturer, originated 'Courtauld crape': the mourning crepe worn

by women in the 1890s. This triumph of branding reinforced the sartorial component of mourning etiquette and enabled Courtaulds to dominate the *crape anglaise* market for approximately 50 years.

One theory for the traditional popularity of crepe in mourning wear is that its dull, unostentatious and non-reflective surface makes it particularly appropriate for public bereavement. Even now, crepe isn't typically embellished with velvet, satin, lace or embroidery. Another advantage of the tradition of using crepe for mourning wear was that its tightly twisted texture made it a low-maintenance and virtually crease-resistant fabric, cutting down on laundering and ironing when a grieving woman might most want to avoid the extra work.

During the first half of the twentieth century, fabric manufacturers experimented extensively with synthetic yarns such as nylon and polyester. These man-made materials have greater durability as well as superior stain- and weather-resistance when compared to natural fibres; however, they are also less ventilated and often irritate sensitive skin. One pioneer of synthetic fibres was Dennis Hibbert, chief textile engineer at Chesline and Crepes Sutton Mills in Macclesfield. Hibbert established that boiling synthetic fibres could subdue their irritating properties. This discovery led to the development of a crepe-like material derived from Terylene, a resin of the polyester family: Crimplene. The patent for Crimplene was subsequently sold to Imperial Chemical Industries (ICI), a transaction that also explains the material's name: Crimplene is said to be a reference to the Crimple Valley, which is near ICI's headquarters in Harrogate; 'crimp' also means (conveniently) 'to press or fold into fine waves' – i.e., to achive the very texture of crepe.

*This simple turquoise crepe jacket in lightweight Holland & Sherry challis with one-button closure, slant-jetted pockets and peak lapel epitomizes summer.*

The chairman of ICI, Sir Paul Chambers, was a regular customer of my old Huntsman mentor Colin Hammick, and one day in the 1960s he brought into Huntsman a length of Crimplene that he asked Hammick, Brian Hall and our trusty trousers cutter Dick Lakey to make up into some sample suits. The result was 'The Easy Suit in Crimplene for Men', an essentially wrinkle-proof ensemble with a belt, long collar and razor-sharp pleats, finished off with a scarf or cravat. Hammick's Easy Suit stole the show on countless runways, along with another Crimplene opus: a white suit with black facing that resembled a reverse dinner jacket. Owing to its clean lines and convenient 'wash-and-wear' qualities, Crimplene became hugely popular, indeed synonomous with the time – until the mid-1970s, when it was supplanted by fabrics with greater ease of movement and ventilation. Eventually, sartorial tastes circled back to favour a higher concentration of natural fibres, resulting in a preponderance of synthetic and natural-fibre blends that unite the most advantageous qualities of both.

*Above: Victorian widow in black silk mourning crepe,* c. *1880. Opposite:*
*A model wearing a blue-and-white pinstriped Crimplene suit at the*
*Crimplene for Men Show, London, 1969.*

Today, there are approximately 80 different kinds of crepe, ranging from aerophane to yeddo, and after contemplating its mourning-wear history it is something of a marvel to behold the brilliant turquoise Holland & Sherry challis iteration you see here. A Super 140 Merino wool fabric with a fine, crisp handle and weighing only 7.5 ounces (215 grams), this crepe is a true lightweight material for warm weather. But with its dense weave – its unusual appearance is achieved by spinning the yarn with a much higher number of S- or Z-direction twists than in ordinary yarn – such fine crepe also performs excellently. As with seersucker (*see pages 38–43*) its inherent tension makes it virtually crease-resistant: you can scrunch it up in a ball and it will spring back to look smooth as new.

Often at Richard Anderson we feature a garment in a bold colour in order to draw customers' attention to the garment itself, with the result being that a majority of customers decide they do indeed want the garment, but in a tamer, more traditional hue. Not in this case. When we showed customers this simple single-breasted jacket, it was all about the colour. Turquoise exudes the essence of summer – so much so that in many cases we gave the coat what is called a buggy lining, which covers only the top half of the inside of the coat, minimizing the coat's weight and keeping it as cool and aerated as possible. In addition to turquoise, this crepe by Holland & Sherry comes in cobalt, lavender, primrose and green – all vibrant colours, and about as far away on the spectrum from mourning black as you can get.

*Above: Advert for Crimplene mens' club jackets in* Punch *magazine, 10 November 1965.*

*Above: The clean simplicity of the jacket carries through in details such as the 3-inch peaked lapel with swelled stitching ¼-inch from the edge (top) and the working one-button cuff with a smoke-pearl button (inset).*

# SINGLE-BREASTED LILAC GABARDINE ASYMMETRIC COAT

A s the saying goes: in order to break the rules you need to learn them first.

In the early 1980s, during my apprentice days at Huntsman, one of my jobs was to assist every Friday in the passing of coats from the workshop upstairs down to fitting room No. 5. This was where master cutter Colin Hammick would 'pass' – or not pass – each of the coats I'd brought down. Some of the coats would have been basted for a first fitting; the majority, however, were 'forwards' (advance fittings) and 'finishes' (finished coats) from the Heddon Street workshop. In order to assess each coat, Hammick would do an impressive corporal impersonation of the

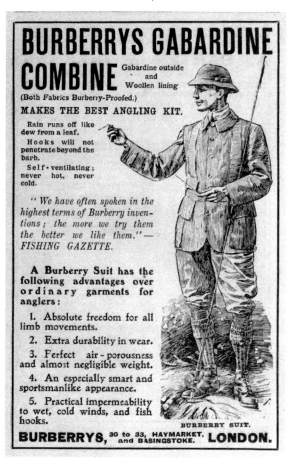

**BURBERRYS GABARDINE**

**COMBINE** Gabardine outside and Woollen lining
(Both Fabrics Burberry-Proofed.)

**MAKES THE BEST ANGLING KIT.**

Rain runs off like dew from a leaf.

Hooks will not penetrate beyond the barb.

Self-ventilating; never hot, never cold.

*" We have often spoken in the highest terms of Burberry inventions; the more we try them the better we like them."— FISHING GAZETTE.*

A Burberry Suit has the following advantages over ordinary garments for anglers:

1. Absolute freedom for all limb movements.

2. Extra durability in wear.

3. Perfect air-porousness and almost negligible weight.

4. An especially smart and sportsmanlike appearance.

5. Practical impermeability to wet, cold winds, and fish hooks.

BURBERRY SUIT.

**BURBERRYS,** 30 to 33, HAYMARKET, and BASINGSTOKE. **LONDON.**

customer, imitating to the best of his ability the client's stance and size. If the client had broad shoulders, for example, Hammick would stand tall and inhale deeply to expand his own modest chest. If the customer tended to slouch, Hammick would roll his shoulders forward and lower his head. And if he deemed the garment ready to be fitted on the customer, Hammick would 'pass' it into the hanging room; if not, well, back up to the Heddon Street workshop for alterations it went. My role, in addition to couriering all these clothes to and fro, was to observe Hammick's appraisals keenly. I was to learn everything I could not only from his technical acumen but also from his work ethic, his unflagging aspiration to perfection.

One day, Hammick was trying on a coat made for one of our especially fastidious customers: an Iranian man whom we were all instructed to refer to as 'His Excellency'. Just before passing the coat, Hammick made a comment undoubtedly designed to keep me on my toes: 'Young Richard,' he said slyly. 'Do you notice anything unusual about this coat?' After looking it up and down and side to side, I admitted that I could identify nothing out of sorts; in other words, I failed my test miserably. For there was something unusual about the coat: its outbreast pocket, which you would usually find on the left-hand side of a coat, here had been sewn on the right. The customer wasn't left-handed; he simply liked his outbreast pocket this way, as a sort of calling card – a purely idiosyncratic request. To my eye, the coat did look slightly odd and unbalanced; moreover (in my defence) I was looking not at the coat itself but at its reflection in a mirror. Still, I wasn't yet seasoned enough to spot the difference immediately. Once I did, with Hammick's help, the detail lodged in my mind, and I've been musing over the sartorial potential of rule-breaking ever since.

*Advertisement for Burberry waterproof gabardine angling suit, 1908.*

*Intentionally 'wrong' details that catch the eye in this already eye-catching lilac gabardine jacket include the outbreast wet pocket on the wearer's right, rather than usual left, side (above); and an asymmetric lapel that is single-breasted, 3½-inch notched on the right side (above) and double-breasted, 4¼-inch peaked on the left side (opposite right).*

In 2012, when it came time to choose some summer fabrics, we selected a gabardine from Dormeuil in two estival colours: stone and lilac. Since the Middle Ages, the word 'gabardine' (or 'gaberdine') has been understood to mean a long, loose outer garment with wide sleeves. (In Shakespeare's *The Merchant of Venice*, for example, Shylock is described as wearing a 'Jewish gaberdine'.) In later centuries, the term referred to any kind of cloak, pinafore, smock-frock or cassock one might wear in wet weather, and it was in this spirit that Thomas Burberry, in 1879, gave the name gabardine to the tightly woven,

waterproofed twill that he developed and which was patented in 1888. In the early twentieth century, its durability, porousness, and virtual impermeability to water, wind and even fish hooks made Burberry's gabardine a popular choice for 'angling kit' and the clothes worn by polar or mountain explorers including Ernest Shackleton and George Mallory. By the 1950s, however, gabardine was more typically used in the making-up of suits, overcoats, windbreakers and colourful, casual jackets like the model you see here.

Except in one respect. To showcase Dormeuil's exquisite lilac gabardine, I decided finally to take what I'd learned back in Huntsman's fitting room No. 5 one step further. Not only did I move the outbreast pocket to the right side, as Hammick's Iranian customer used to like; I also gave the coat one single-breasted notched lapel and one double-breasted peaked lapel. We chose a matching lilac Ermazine lining (as ever, with any unusual colour or texture you don't want to overdo it) and then we put it in our shop window and sat back to wait. It wasn't long before people walking by stopped, furrowed their brows and in some cases even came in to ask if we were aware that something was 'wrong' with the coat in our window. Interestingly – like myself 30 years earlier – they all knew something was off, but they couldn't quite put their fingers on what it was.

I enjoyed this minor apostasy, which, after all, became a talking point and drew attention to Dormeuil's sublime material. We wound up selling dozens of coats in lilac gabardine – which, incidentally, tends to look best on darker skin tones; on someone with a very pale complexion it can make the wearer look washed-out. And we sold at least ten asymmetrical models as well, not only in the gabardine but also in other colours and materials, including one

*Above: The asymmetry and unusual colour of the coat are offset by simple, classic details such as the one-button closure and straight jetted pockets. Opposite: Twill surface texture of the Dormueil lilac gabardine.*

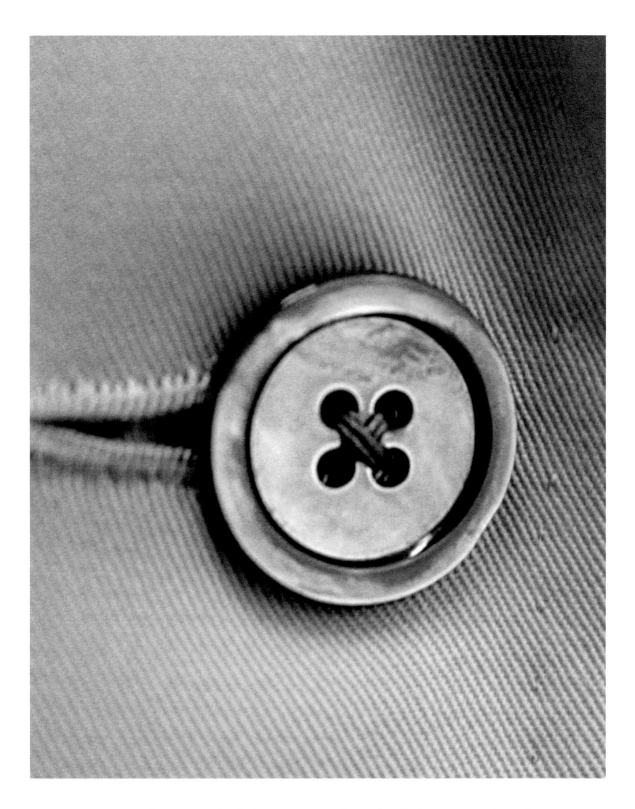

in 'Harvey check' (*see pages 88–93*) to a dentist in San Francisco. The coat's
offbeat style seems to appeal in particular to members of the music industry,
including two rap artists whom I count among my clientele. They like it,
I suppose, because it has something rebellious about it, an inventive audacity
that makes you look twice. One doesn't want to tamper with tradition too often
or too radically, of course – no one aspires to turn Savile Row into Cartoonland
– but a little whimsy never hurt anyone, and sometimes it can even have
a welcome, exhilarating effect.

# SINGLE-BREASTED CREAM LINEN WAISTCOAT

The waistcoat, or 'vest' in American parlance, is a sleeveless upper-body garment that has been around in various forms since the Restoration era, when it was supposedly inspired by the Persian vests English visitors observed in the court of Shah Abbas. The garment's name probably derives from the practice of cutting the piece at waist level, compared to the considerably longer length to which coats with sleeves were cut during this period. There are at least two alternative theories regarding the origin of the term 'waistcoat', both less likely but informative and entertaining nonetheless. One is that such vests were made from material left over from the cutting of a two-piece suit – thus 'waste-coat', a garment created to avoid wastage. Another recalls that during the seventeenth century military men wore 'wastecoats' that were the reverse colour of their overcoats, and that these vests were made by turning old overcoats inside-out and cutting off the sleeves – again, to minimize wastage. Whatever the term's origin, there has been an upsurge in interest in the waistcoat over the last five or six years, interest attributable at least in part to the popularity of period television dramas such as *Mad Men*, about the advertising industry in New York in the 1950s and 60s, and *Peaky Blinders*, a crime drama set in Birmingham, England, in the years immediately following the First World War. There have also been many second-hand shops springing up of late, and this too has contributed to a trend toward vintage-minded fashion, of which the waistcoat seems to be a universally recognized trademark. One can even cite the influence of Gary Barlow, who made a habit of wearing a waistcoat as a judge on the British television programme *The X Factor*, and who has been mentioned to me by more than one customer wanting a waistcoat of his own – turning our collective consciousness back to the eras of martini lunches, spats and even pocketwatches.

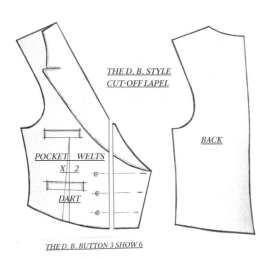

THE D. B. STYLE CUT-OFF LAPEL

BACK

POCKET WELTS
X  2

DART

THE D. B. BUTTON 3 SHOW 6

For a garment relatively limited in its size and shape, the waistcoat has evolved considerably over the years, from the elaborate, brightly coloured models of the seventeenth and eighteenth centuries to the more sober versions of the nineteenth and the informal lounge-suit enhancer of the twentieth. When I worked at Huntsman, waistcoats were a staple, and while you can make them in virtually any fabric, one of our most popular was the plain linen variety you see here. One reason for its longstanding popularity is its flexibility: you can wear a plain linen waistcoat to Ascot or to a wedding, under a morning coat or with a black coat and trousers – really, it complements any suiting combination. We like to use an Irish linen from W. Bill or Holland & Sherry, which, at 10–12 ounces (285–340 grams), creases slightly and performs well. The most common colour for odd or singular waistcoats has

*Pattern illustration showing forepart and back for a double-breasted waistcoat.*

long been dove grey, but over the years I've come to prefer the soft cream of this model, which to my eye looks fresher, zippier and, well, more modern. Most of the waistcoats we make are collarless, though some men prefer a notched lapel like the one you see here. Just like a regular lounge coat, a waistcoat can be single- or double-breasted – the latter, as ever, being more formal, whereas a single-breasted waistcoat works just as well with a lounge suit or even jeans. At Richard Anderson we tend to give our double-breasted waistcoat six buttons – three on each side – and a bowed, which is to say slightly curved, lapel. By contrast, the classic single-breasted version is what we call 'button five show six,' which means it has six buttons all in a row, with the bottom one typically left undone. This custom was allegedly popularized by the Prince of Wales, who either routinely forgot to do up his last button or was merely accommodating an expanding waistline. In either case, leaving the bottom button undone helps a waistcoat retain it shape and prevents it from riding up on the body when the wearer sits down, which is perhaps why the practice has endured.

To create a waistcoat, you convert a customer's existing coat pattern by removing the sleeves, of course, but also in a way that brings the garment

*Above: The single-breasted cream waistcoat is made in the 'button five show six' style, with four welted pockets and a notched lapel. Opposite: Cillian Murphy wearing a waistcoat in television drama* Peaky Blinders.

closer to the waist and chest, while also preserving its comfort and balance. First the back must be manipulated and swung such that it hugs the shoulder blades and lower back. Then the scye (armhole) is split and lowered to gain the side seam run, the front edge of the forepart is reduced, and the front shoulder is picked up at the neck point. The waistcoat's length is dictated by the customer's hipbone, with the finished length at the side seam on or just below the bone, and running down to a shaped front point. In approximately 75% of cases a waistcoat has a strap with a buckle on the back, used to pull the waistcoat even snugger; in the other 25% the waisting effect is achieved instead with a permanent dart. It is relatively easy to adjust a waistcoat: we typically make them with a little inlay in the back lining, so if a client gains in circumference we can let out the inlay and, if there is one, extend the strap.

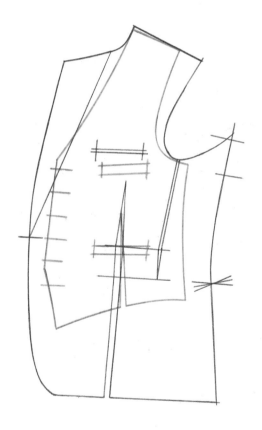

COAT TO WAISTCOAT CONVERSION

In my Huntsman days, Colin Hammick used to wear a black striped suit with a single-breasted cream waistcoat to work. The company's many waistcoat fans included Gregory Peck (who wore one in most of his scenes in *To Kill A Mockingbird; see page 41*) as well as Terry Thomas, Peter Sellers, Stewart Granger, Peter Ustinov and Frederick Seidel. Huntman's owner Edward Packer also loved waistcoats and had an unusual model designed for him by Brian Hall: seen here in brown plaid, it had a low scooped front and three buttons, and was cut straight across the bottom, which discouraged it from riding up.

Much more recently, I made the rap artist Chipmunk a waistcoat for his twenty-first birthday party. Usually the back of a waistcoat is made of silk or another lining-appropriate material that matches the waistcoat's front, but in Chipmunk's case the front was white linen and the back black Ermazine, which we also used for the waistcoat's welts. And to finish it off? White pearl buttons. Indeed, a waistcoat can be an effective way to inject a bit of personality into a wardrobe; for some fans, wearing one is even a daily habit. We once took an order from a Swiss financier who wanted four linen waistcoats made up all at once: in cream, khaki, yellow and blue. I imagine he can be seen wearing one more often than not – the way some men wear a tie.

*Above: Pattern illustration showing the conversion from coat forepart to waistcoat forepart.*

*Above: Waistcoat back made from cream Ermazine (top) and cream
Ermazine back strap positioned at the natural waist (inset).*

61

# MINT-GREEN
# CASH-COT
# SAFARI COAT

The safari coat was originally conceived in the early twentieth century as a practical garment to be worn by soldiers in warm climates, or by adventurers exploring the African bush. It was also famously modelled by swashbucklers from Theodore Roosevelt to Ernest Hemingway, who reportedly commissioned his own version from the expeditionary outfitters Willis & Geiger. In the 1960s, the safari coat experienced something of a renaissance after French designers including Yves Saint Laurent reconceived its big-cat hunter's look for the catwalk. Its popularity grew even more when Roger Moore wore versions as James Bond in *The Man with the Golden Gun* (1974), *Moonraker* (1979) and *Octopussy* (1983). The first time I saw a safari coat in the flesh it was being modelled by the

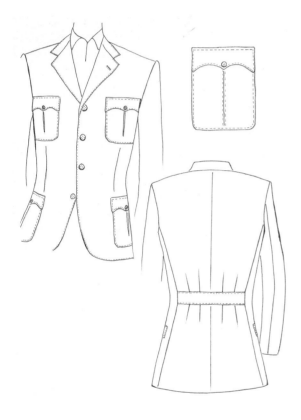

British soldier and travel writer Sir Patrick Leigh Fermor, a.k.a. Paddy, who was a friend of Colin Hammick and ordered several safari coats from Huntsman over the years. And then there was Geoffrey Kent, another Huntsman client and founder of the international luxury safari broker Abercrombie & Kent, who also helped to ensure the safari coat became a staple at No. 11 – as were safari shirts, a lighter version that offered many of the same practical features but could be worn alone. Stewart Granger wore a Huntsman safari coat in the film *Bhowani Junction* (1956), as did Virginia McKenna in *Born Free* (1966).

By the dawn of the new millennium, however, the safari coat's popularity had waned. Certainly I got the sense that many of our younger customers saw it – and certainly the shirt – as a touch old-fashioned. Done well, however, the safari coat can be a practical and valuable addition to any wardrobe, being sporty, durable and endowed with spacious storage in the form of the roomy 'bellows' pockets that give it its military slant. Accordingly, I set to thinking about how we might update it for the twenty-first century.

Once again, revival of a tradition came in the form of a non-traditional colour. Typically made of a lightweight cotton, linen or poplin, safari coats normally come in a neutral shade such as stone, fawn or beige – otherwise known to the more military-minded as khaki. A light yellow-brownish colour whose name derives from the Persian *khâk*, meaning 'soil,' khaki is a common choice for the uniforms of military personnel (or spies) wishing to camouflage themselves in the jungle or desert. Civilians, however, particularly fashion-conscious ones, tend not to mind being visible, so when I was reviewing some cash-cot corduroy samples from our supplier Zegna one day and a distinctly

*Original working fashion sketch for the cash-cot safari coat showing four-button front, half belt and darts to back, as well as pocket details.*

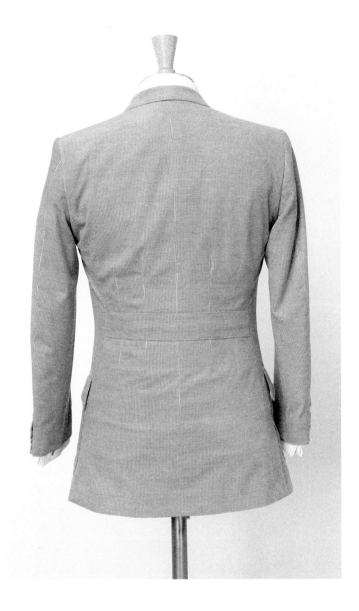

modern mint-green swatch caught my eye, I thought 'Why not?' 'Cash-cot' is shorthand for a cashmere-cotton blend, in this case at a light 9-ounce (255-gram) weight that I immediately recognized as one that would marry up well with the safari coat's sultry-weather look. In fact, I had long had it in the back of my mind to make a safari coat in Moygashel, a brand name that for many years was synonymous with a high-quality Irish linen that has the most beautiful natural slubs and crease. Customers often came into Huntsman wanting something made of linen, but, as I have said, Colin Hammick and Brian Hall were so disinclined to work with lightweight material (because it didn't flatter the Huntsman line) that they would even go so far as to suggest the customer take his order elsewhere. Moygashel, however, offered a compromise: it *looked* like linen but acted more like wool, and therefore Hammick and Hall were willing to use it. Unfortunately, true Moygashel is impossible to come by these days – yet when I held Zegna's cash-cot samples in my hand I was able to imagine the material behaving in a similarly light yet shape-retaining way. The result would be a more

*Above: Back view of the coat, showing half belt with two darts either side. Opposite: This safari coat for the urban explorer is faithful to the practicality of the more rugged original, made from a lightweight cash-cot Zegna fabric that looks like linen but holds its shape like wool.*

*Roger Moore (with Britt Ekland, right, and Maud Adams, left) wearing a safari coat as James Bond in* The Man With The Golden Gun *(1974).*

luxurious-feeling (and looking) but still practical safari coat, tweaked ever so slightly for the purpose of city wear. Since then, we have also done a few safari coats in navy, as well as one in an oatmeal linen with a contrasting saddle stitch in claret. But it was the mint-green version that seemed to get people's attention – that really made the garment 'pop'. And thus a new generation of Savile Row enthusiasts was introduced to the safari coat's unique union of practicality and romanticism.

The safari coat is traditionally a short, straight jacket, cinched at the waist by a belt. I tend to cut mine a little longer than the standard: to a length equal with the bottom of the customer's suit jacket. I do this to avoid

crowding the coat's four vertically arranged buttons and also to accommodate the four large pockets that characterize its front. Sewn onto the outside of the coat, these pockets are called bellows pockets because they have an expansion pleat reminiscent of an accordion's bellows. They are by far the trickiest part of making up a safari coat, as getting the folds symmetrically just so is an unusual feat for cutter and tailor alike. Originally designed to hold binoculars, compasses, cameras, pistols, guidebooks, canteens, ammunition and all other manner of equipment a trailblazer might need in the savannah, bellows pockets are so big that if you cut the coat too short it can start to look all pockets and no coat. Another distinguishing feature of the safari coat is its clean, streamlined arms; I also make my models more fitted around the waist (by putting a dart in either side), such that the belt is superficial, really. You can also do away with the belt altogether, as Hemingway did, or opt for a half belt, though this of course makes for a somewhat less formal look.

Soon after we made up our first mint-green version and featured it on a sales trip to the United States, we quickly sold about a dozen or so over a period of two years (2005–06). For our semiannual 'Look Book', the actor Enzo Cilenti modelled one over grey trousers, a black rollneck and burgundy tasselled loafers (*see page 65*). A safari coat also looks great with grey trousers and a polo shirt – or, like my under-35 customers, you can dress it down with a t-shirt and jeans. It's a long way from the colonialist look sported by Teddy Roosevelt back in 1909 – and these days bellows pockets are more likely to contain an iPhone than a compass – but the adventuresome spirit of the safari coat still endures.

*The military-style outbreast bellows pocket, with a four-hole smoke-pearl button, perfect for stowing a compass – or an iPhone.*

# DOUBLE-BREASTED NAVY BLUE CASHMERE-SILK DRESSING GOWN

Why didn't I keep it? It was used to me and I was used to it. It moulded all the folds of my body without inhibiting it; I was picturesque and handsome ... I was the absolute master of my old robe.
    – Denis Diderot, 'Regrets for my Old Dressing Gown' (1769)

Once upon a time, it was not only common but even presumed that when a man came home from work (or play) at the end of the day he would slip a dressing gown on over his shirt and trousers or pyjamas, even if it was just for an hour or so, before dressing again for an evening event. This tradition of men wearing dressing gowns dates back to at least the seventeenth century and was likely inspired by Eastern versions such as Persian or Indian robes or the Japanese kimono. By the 1860s, dressing gowns largely resembled those of today, with a long shawl collar plunging to a belted waist. Hugh Bonneville was often seen wearing a dressing gown as Lord Grantham in the hugely popular period television drama *Downton Abbey*, and dressing gowns ranging from the plain to the resplendent have appeared on countless other actors in television programmes and films over the years, including Leslie Howard in *Pygmalion* (1938), Monty Woolley in *The Man Who Came to Dinner* (1942), Claude Rains in *Deception* (1946), Robert Walker in *Strangers on a Train* (1951), Alfred Molina in *Boogie Nights* (1997), Frank Langella in *Lolita* (1997), and Benedict Cumberbatch in *Sherlock* (2010–).

Sadly, owing at least in part to modern improvements in indoor heating, the dressing gown is a rare statement today; people tend to relax at home in cotton or terrycloth robes, or in casual clothing with no robe at all. But at Huntsman well into the 1980s we made as many as six dressing gowns a year, with both Mr Hammick and Mr Hall excelling in the garment's relaxed elegance. The most common fabric chosen for such a garment was cashmere, but occasionally a customer would order one in superluxurious vicuña, or doeskin. Typically the chosen fabric would be only 10–11 ounces (285–310 grams), as by this time dressing gowns were worn rather more for luxury than for warmth. Dark blue was the most popular colour, though we did also make gowns in fawn and pale grey. Generally, a dressing gown has a plain back, like that on a duffel coat, and is square-fronted with the aforementioned shawl collar. It would have a belt about 1¾ inches wide,

*Our navy cashmere-silk dressing gown is made in a bold Smith & Woollen's plaid that is also a popular fabric choice for sportcoats.*

usually held in place by loops on either side, and often the belt would
be made of the same material as the gown – although one can of course
choose something different for a bit of contrast. In fact, when it comes to
something that will be worn exclusively in the privacy of one's own home,
I think it's even more common for people to feel that they can personalize
the garment more dramatically than they would something for work or
social occasions. In this spirit, we gave one of our recent dressing-gown
models a chocolate-brown body, with a belt, collar and pockets in burgundy
cashmere. Another bold variation is the model featured here: a blue Smith
& Woollen's plaid with a large overcheck in red, navy and yellow, a matching
belt, and pockets, pointed cuffs and collar in navy. We have made quite
a few sportcoats in this same plaid material – which, incidentally, is one
of our most popular fabrics.

   A dressing gown is not nearly as fitted as a coat, of course, so in cutting
one you can relax the customer's usual coat pattern a little, adding ¼ inch
or so across the back, as well as affording a straighter side seam and an
easier, fuller sleeve and scye. We would also lighten the construction, still
using a full syddo canvas through the front but with felt only at the chest,

*Original working fashion sketch showing contrasting navy, red and
yellow cashmere-silk large overcheck plaid against navy trim.*

*Monty Woolley wearing a classic dressing gown in the film* The Man
Who Came to Dinner *(1942).*

as opposed to felt on top of horsehair. A lightweight shoulder pad is also essential. Normally, we would make our own pads, with the average coat pad involving 2 ½ plys of wadding, the canvas inserted and shaped accordingly. In our dressing gowns, by contrast, just one ply with soft canvas suffices. The waist position is higher and the length longer than those on a standard lounge coat, of course, and the dressing gown also has a larger wrap (i.e., the amount of material that overlaps in the front), making the conversion process somewhat similar to that of changing a single-breasted overcoat pattern to a double-breasted one.

Colin Hammick was not only a great gown-cutter but also a great gown-wearer, his pride and joy being a navy cashmere with wine cording along the edge. The cashmere was a gift to him from one of his favourite customers, an art dealer who resided in Seattle. Every three months or so the gown would be grandly brought from his flat in Pelham Court to be hand-pressed by Michael Grainger on our first-floor workshop. Unfortunately, disaster was to strike: when arriving back at work on a Monday morning in the late 1980s we discovered broken windows and a complete theft of all of the garments that had been left on the workroom's rails over the weekend. To make their escape via Heddon Street, the thieves had fled over the Savile Row workshops, dropping a dozen or so garments as they did. Sadly, Mr Hammick's 'Old Friend' was not among them. A remake was duly booked but alas the sentimental value of the replacement was obviously not the same.

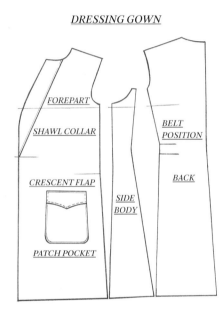

*DRESSING GOWN*

FOREPART

SHAWL COLLAR

BELT POSITION

CRESCENT FLAP

BACK

SIDE BODY

PATCH POCKET

This wasn't our only dressing-gown drama. Hammick once took an order for a dressing gown in a deluxe vicuña picked out by a one G. Kostelitz; the fabric was so expensive that for the basting stage Hammick brought up some old tweed that had been lying in the Hunstman cellar for years and basted together a toile of the coat using that. Then, at some point between the basting-up and fitting stage, we had a house sale, in which old leftover bits of fabric were sold off to the staff. The rest of the fabric that Hammick had used for Kostelitz's baste was sold to a tailoress intending to make a bunch of tweed skirts. Then Kostelitz came in and tried on the baste version and … loved it! He wanted *two* dressing gowns, one for him and one for Mrs Kostelitz, in the same tweed material Hammick had used for the baste in addition to the one in the luxurious vicuña he'd already chosen. At which point Hammick had to go reluctantly, cap in hand, to our long-serving tailoress Pam, who shrewdly charged him quadruple to buy back the fabric. But Kostelitz got his gowns.

*Above: Pattern illustration for the dressing gown showing forepart, side-body and back. Opposite: The dressing gown has a shawl collar (top), crescent-shaped turn-back cuffs and patch pockets with crescent-shaped flap and an angled 1¾-inch tied belt (inset).*

# STRONG

# SUITS

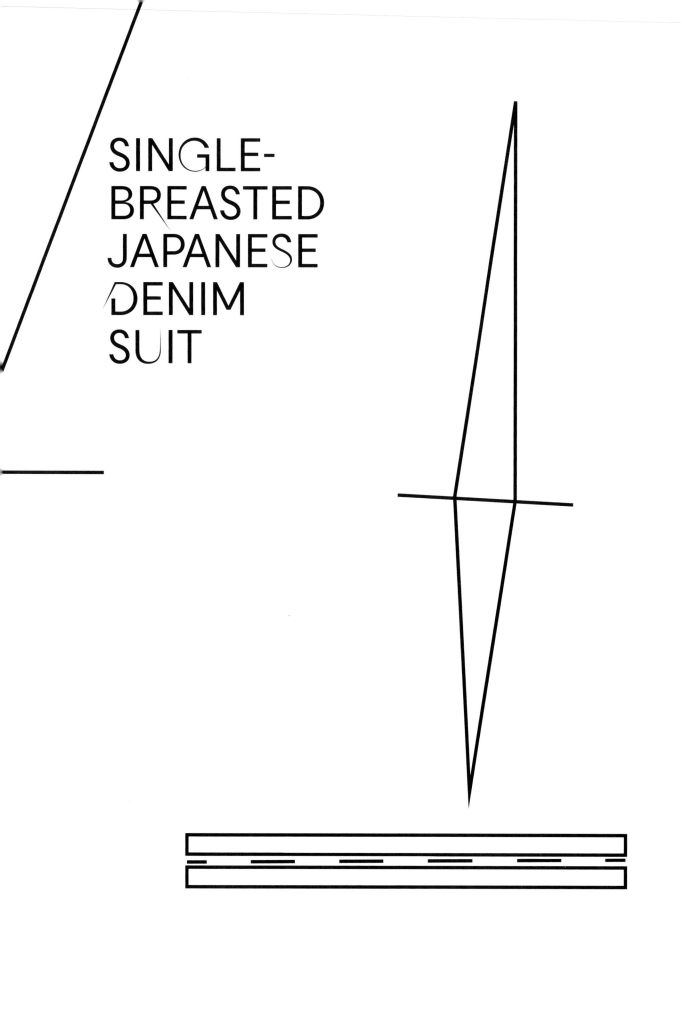

SINGLE-
BREASTED
JAPANESE
DENIM
SUIT

L egend has it that in 1873 a Nevada tailor by the name of Jacob Davis was asked by a local woman to make her husband a sturdy pair of work trousers in which he could chop wood. Davis accepted the commission, and, just before finishing the heavy canvas legwear, was inspired to reinforce its pockets with some copper rivets he'd had lying around. Soon, the popularity of Davis's handiwork spread, and, recognizing an opportunity, Davis wrote a proposal to the dry goods wholesaler Levi Strauss & Co. to mass produce his rivet-reinforced work trousers. The original material used by Levi's tended to chafe, however, so in due course the company substituted a twilled cotton cloth called *serge de Nîmes*, after

the French city of Nîmes, where the softer material was made. And thus the term 'denim' came into common parlance, from *de Nîmes*; and, in similar fashion, the word 'jeans', from the French name for Genoa, *Gênes*, whose sailors typically wore clothes of the same indigo hue.

Fast-forward nearly 150 years and, notwithstanding the French and American origins of blue jeans, today it is in Japan that the world's best-quality denim is made. The story of Japanese denim started with the American love affair with jeans, encouraged by James Dean wearing them in the film *Rebel Without a Cause* (1955). At the time Japan was immersed in its own love affair with American culture. Numerous Japanese companies sprang up to emulate the clothing and style of American stars; simultaneously, American companies were abandoning traditional denim shuttle looms in favour of the wider and more economical projectile ones. A few of the old shuttle looms crossed the seas and the foundations of the Japanese denim industry were laid, such that today for the truly authentic article you have to go to Kurashiki.

Traditional shuttle looms weave using a continuous cross-thread (the weft) that is passed on a shuttle back and forth along the length of the bolt. As the thread loops around to make its return journey, it creates a self-edge, or 'selvedge', the feature that differentiates traditional shuttle-loom denim from the more modern, selvedge-less variety. Japanese companies improved the weaving processes but retained the selvedge, which is now a mark of 'true' denim. A distinctly sturdy cotton twill – two or more white weft threads pass under a dyed warp thread, yielding a cloth with a ribbed texture dark on one side and light on the other – denim is traditionally dyed its signature indigo, but is available in an almost

*James Dean wearing his iconic denim jeans in the film* Rebel Without a Cause *(1955).*

*Above: Navy polka-dot Ermazine lining is the one flamboyant detail
in the otherwise simple, classic jacket.*

*Above: Made of denim from Japanese company Betty Smith, the suit has a 3⅜-inch notched lapel (top left), three-button cuffs with dark grey horn buttons (bottom left) and straight jetted pockets (bottom right).*

unlimited palette. When I first came across the Japanese version, specifically one produced by a company called Betty Smith, I was so impressed by its lustre and integrity that I immediately wanted to see how it would make up into a bespoke suit. The first consideration was whether we would still be able to put in the shoulders and sleeves by hand. A growing number of coats made today have shoulders and sleeves that have been machined in, but here at No. 13 we try to avoid machining as much as possible (sometimes it is inevitable, particularly with very heavy material, such as the pink-dyed melton used for hunting coats). So I was delighted to discover that while the

Japanese denim was heavy, at 15 ounces (425 grams), it was still supple enough to be hand-stitched. When we compared the look of a handmade shoulder to a machined one, the verdict was clear: the old-fashioned way won out.

As for the rest of design: I kept it simple, because I wanted the material to speak for itself. The jacket has just one button, a regular notched collar and a classic cut. The trousers have a slightly narrower leg. We kept it simple, really; no point in gilding the lily. The only flourish we decided to give our denim suit was a navy with white polka-dot lining. There are so many denim fans out there that we've made at least 30 such suits since I cut my very first one back in 2006.

Our clients invariably report that the material only gets better the more it is worn: denim takes time to settle in and is at its best after it's been exposed to all four seasons. Denim has a way of coming to feel like a good friend. Creases develop around the arms, and, because indigo dye doesn't penetrate to the core of the fibres, abrasion causes the colour to wear off over time, giving the material that slightly faded, lived-in look. A slightly worn-in denim suit looks fabulous at a cocktail party; it can be dressed up with a tie and a bright white shirt or down with a t-shirt; my New York customers like to combine it with a rollneck sweater, a handkerchief, a scarf and maybe a pair of suede shoes – denim is a way of fending off those Nor'easter winds while still managing to look hip. A denim suit does have to be dry-cleaned because the hand-padded canvas and lining need the care of a more formal suit, but in just about every other respect it's as low-maintenance as formalwear gets.

*Above: Fashion sketch showing styling and colour figuration of ageing/ worn denim. Opposite: The denim suit jacket can be paired with a tie and a white shirt for a hip, yet formal look.*

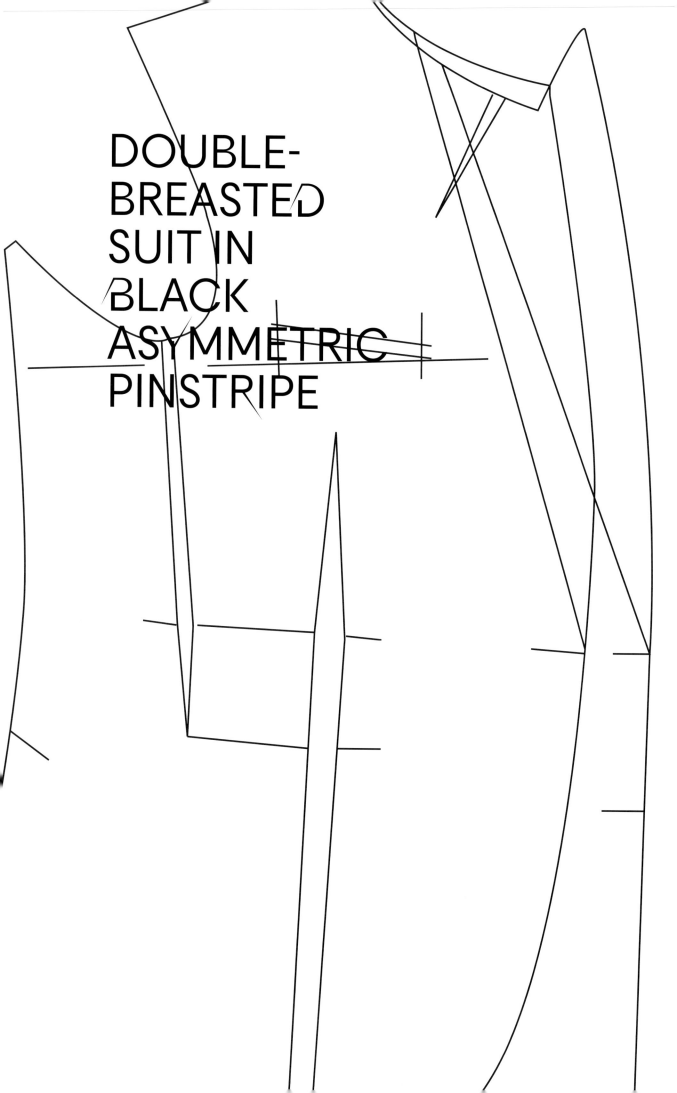

DOUBLE-
BREASTED
SUIT IN
BLACK
ASYMMETRIC
PINSTRIPE

n 2001, in the months leading up to the moment when we would first open Richard Anderson Ltd, Brian and I visited several mills in search of the perfect materials with which to launch our new enterprise. In short, we wanted to be able to offer our customers a unique material that looked both classic and contemporary. Ideally, it would be a fabric that managed to transcend the old, dark tweed-and-staghead trappings of the historic houses on Savile Row while also having an aesthetic deeply rooted in quality and tradition. And the eventual upshot of our brainstorming was a fresh take on one of suiting's most time-honoured motifs: the pinstripe.

The origins of the pinstripe remain debatable. One theory is that it derives from banking uniforms, which had distinctive stripes to identify the employees of each different bank. Another theory involves the long-established trend of athletic attire influencing everyday wear: specifically, the adaptation of the boating uniforms of the nineteenth century into clothing that could be worn to the office. Light stripes on a dark background have long been viewed as more formal, whereas dark stripes against a light background have a more casual, sporty look evocative of ball games, racetracks and cocktails on the lawn. Striping has also long featured on the inside of suits as well: in many West End tailoring houses it has been customary to line a suit's sleeves with a distinctive 'house stripe', such as the burgundy-and-cream striped Ermazine that Huntsman sewed into countless sleeves and used as trouser curtains for years.

For our inaugural Richard Anderson pinstripe, we decided on a rather simple idea: taking the traditional up-and-down pinstripe and rotating it about 45 degrees. The stripe would be 'true', which is to say a solid line, rather than the tiny unjoined dots that comprise a 'rain' pinstripe, for example, or the minute braids of a 'cable' stripe, or, indeed, any other standard variation. And the stripe would be narrow-gauge, meaning there would be only ¼ inch or so between each line. Contrary to the usual symmetry of a suit made up of a traditional pinstripe, the two halves of a suit made out of our 'biased' stripe would not be mirror images of each other, but rather would appear 'asymmetrical'. Commissioning a unique fabric with which to make up a limited number of garments is common practice among the bigger houses on Savile Row. Typically it takes only about six weeks from conceptualization to receipt

*At first glance, this is a classic pinstripe suit in a 'button two show three' double-breasted style with straight jetted pockets, but on closer look the pinstripes themselves are intriguingly unique.*

*The unusual diagonal orientation of the pinstripes, and their contrasting angles on facing and forepart, are highlighted in these images.*

of your original material – not too long in bespoke-tailoring terms – and there's a commercial advantage, of course, in that by skipping the middle man and going straight to the fabric-maker you can put what you would have paid a dealer toward the extra cost (if any) of realizing your own design. Above all, there is enormous psychological appeal in originating suiting that is utterly unique and exclusive to you and your customers.

Among our destinations in this pursuit were the mills of Yorkshire, including the high-end manufacturer Moxon Huddersfield, at Yew Tree Mills, Holmbridge. Existing in one form or another for four and half centuries, Moxon is renowned today not only for its long history of producing premium textiles (such as some of the world's finest Merino wool) but also for its enthusiastic production of specially commissioned fabrics. Its more notable designs allegedly include a rainbow-coloured pinstripe commissioned by Richard James on behalf of Elton John, and a gold pinstripe, woven with real gold, for Frank Sinatra. For our own material we chose a Lumbs Golden Bale in 11–12 ounces (310–340 grams) – fabric with an ideal weight for year-round wear and an exceedingly soft handle. We commissioned two lengths (60 metres each), one in navy and one in black, and we made up a suit for each of ourselves – mine the double-breasted black model you see here, Brian's a single-breasted in blue, both with matching plain Ermazine linings. The material proved extremely popular, not only for two-piece suits but also for three-piece ensembles, and while the blue went marginally more quickly we have since sold out of both, now known as 'limited editions'.

These days, we tend to commission approximately two new fabrics every year, though in honour of Brian's sixtieth year as a travelling ambassador of the Row we commissioned a few extra ones in 2016, including some based on fabrics that had been popular sixty years earlier. We will always have a special fondness for our inaugural diagonal pinstripe, however, which helped us to usher in not only a new company and a new century but also a new era of creativity.

*Above: Dark pinstripes on a light ground, as on the uniform worn by American baseball player Walter Johnson in 1925, hint at sporty pursuits. Opposite: Light stripes on a dark ground, as in our original fabric made by Moxon Huddersfield, proclaim classic formality.*

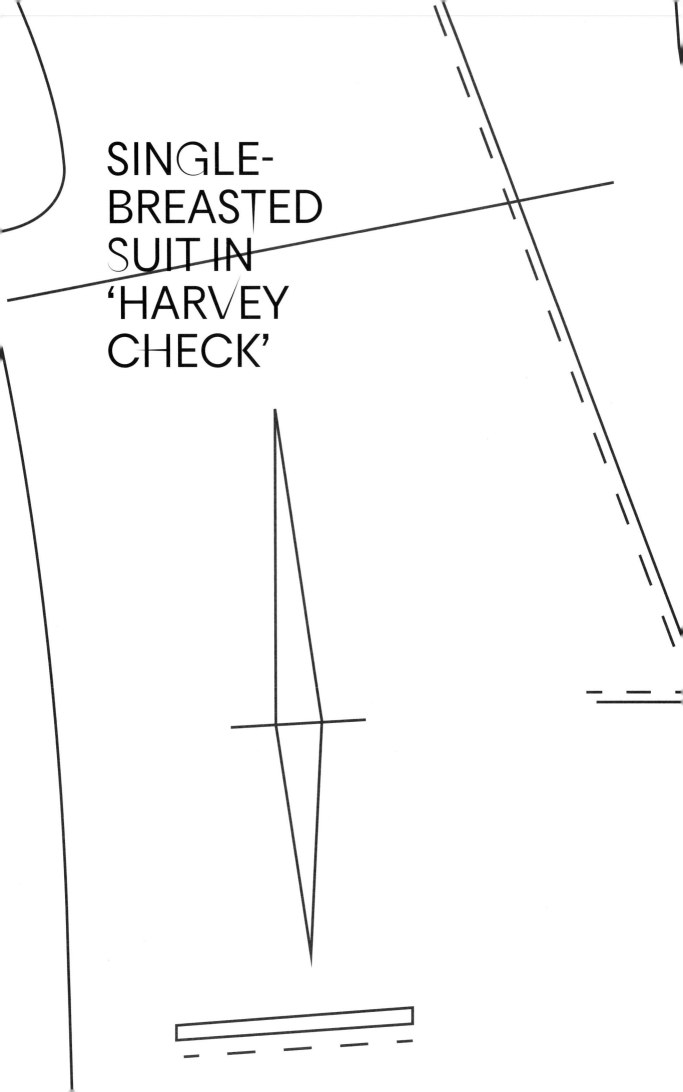

# SINGLE-BREASTED SUIT IN 'HARVEY CHECK'

Perhaps you've heard of a material called Glen check, or Glenurquhart plaid, whose name derives from the Scottish valley of Glen Urquhart? Glen check is a woollen fabric, specifically a woven twill with a pattern of alternating small and large checks. It is sometimes also referred to as Prince of Wales check, popularized as it was by the Duke of Windsor. More recently, variations on the fabric have been seen on the likes of former *Vogue* editor-at-large André Leon Talley, a great wearer of large squares; Cary Grant, who wore a muted blue-and-grey three-button model designed by Kilgour in *North by Northwest* (1959); Pee-Wee Herman, whose infamous too-small uniform came in grey-and-white Glen check;

and Ronald Reagan, whom the press on both sides of the Atlantic deemed 'un-presidential' for wearing a single-breasted, two-button, blue-and-grey Glen plaid suit when he made a tour of Europe in 1982. According to an article in *TIME Magazine* published the same year, the fabric for Reagan's suit, in which he was photographed strolling in the sunshine with Margaret Thatcher, was supplied by the British stockist Illingworth, Morris & Co. Ltd, 'which also furnished the interiors of Rolls Royce autos, the Pope's vestments and the covers for the tennis balls used at Wimbledon'.

Most Glen plaids have what's called an overcheck – the geometric pattern superimposed on the background hue – in red, blue, black or grey. One day in October 2011, however, a customer of ours named J. C. Harvey (a New York-based inventor and decorated Vietnam War veteran) came in to ask if it might be possible to commission a Glen check with an overcheck in a distinctive shade of pale green instead. We took to the idea immediately, and set about commissioning a piece from Steve Willis, of Yorkshire Textiles, to whom we turn for many of the original commissions we order. When the material arrived – a 16-ounce (455-gram) luxury worsted flannel with a heather-grey background and an overcheck in seafoam green – it was beautiful, as expected. And for Mr Harvey we duly made up two suits: one single-breasted coat and trousers, as you see here, and one double-breasted model, both with a lining in matching light green. The minimum order when commissioning an original material from Yorkshire Textiles is 60 metres, which is good for

*Cary Grant wearing a Glen check suit by Kilgour in the Alfred Hitchcock film* North by Northwest *(1959).*

*Above: Our 'Harvey check' version, with heather-grey background and seafoam-green overcheck. Opposite: Glen check worn by the Prince of Wales (later King Edward VII), c. 1880 (top), and by Paul Reubens in* The Pee-Wee Herman Show, *c. 2011 (inset).*

*Top: When working with checks of different hues, a cutter must be careful to orient the darker areas in the same direction and allow enough extra to match the pattern at the seams.*

approximately seventeen or eighteen suits. As of writing, we have made fourteen suits out of our 'Harvey check', leaving just enough material to make three or four more.

There is a cutting issue with any check that features squares of different sizes and hues: you have to cut all pieces of the fabric in the same direction to avoid 'shading'. This is because one half of the check tends to be darker than the other. For example, if you were to cut the front of a pair of trousers out of a piece of Glen check and the back out of the same Glen check, but turned upside-down, the front of the trousers would look darker than the back (or vice versa). Any Savile Row striker who has been taught well will always match the fabric to the pattern such that the dark half of the check is oriented to the top (*see close-up detail of fabric opposite*). This is generally agreed to be the more pleasing aesthetic effect, although to the untrained eye it is perhaps only barely detectable, if at all. Furthermore, to ensure that the lines of the check match up along all seams, you need to add an extra 10 centimetres or so to each pattern edge, for leeway.

The fresh pale green on a Harvey check suit gives it a more contemporary look than its Glenurquhart forerunners, I think. This is precisely because it's a new twist on the form: only in extremely rare cases, if indeed at all, will you see a seafoam-green overcheck on any suits from yesteryear. Indeed, most of our clients who have ordered a Harvey check single- or double-breasted suit have been only in their twenties or thirties – men in search of something a bit 'vintage', that is, a suit that wouldn't have looked entirely out of place in their grandfathers' closets, yet has a certain unprecedented flair that makes it their own. A relatively heavyweight material, Harvey check is perfect for late autumn, winter or early spring. I myself have a special fondness for Harvey check because it reminds me of certain Friday evenings in the early 1980s, when my fellow apprentice Toby and I used to leave Huntsman at the end of the day and head straight to Flip, the famous second-hand clothing shop in Covent Garden. There, we would rummage through the racks looking for something to wear out on the town that very night, spending an hour or more scouring the hundreds of old Glen check suits to find one that fit and could be had for a mere twenty quid. But no, not one of them had an overcheck in seafoam green. Maybe the second-hand clothing shops of the future will.

*Above and opposite inset: The 'Harvey check' suit features a 3-inch notched lapel, one-button fastening and straight jetted pockets for a fresh, contemporary look.*

# ATYPICAL

# TWEEDS

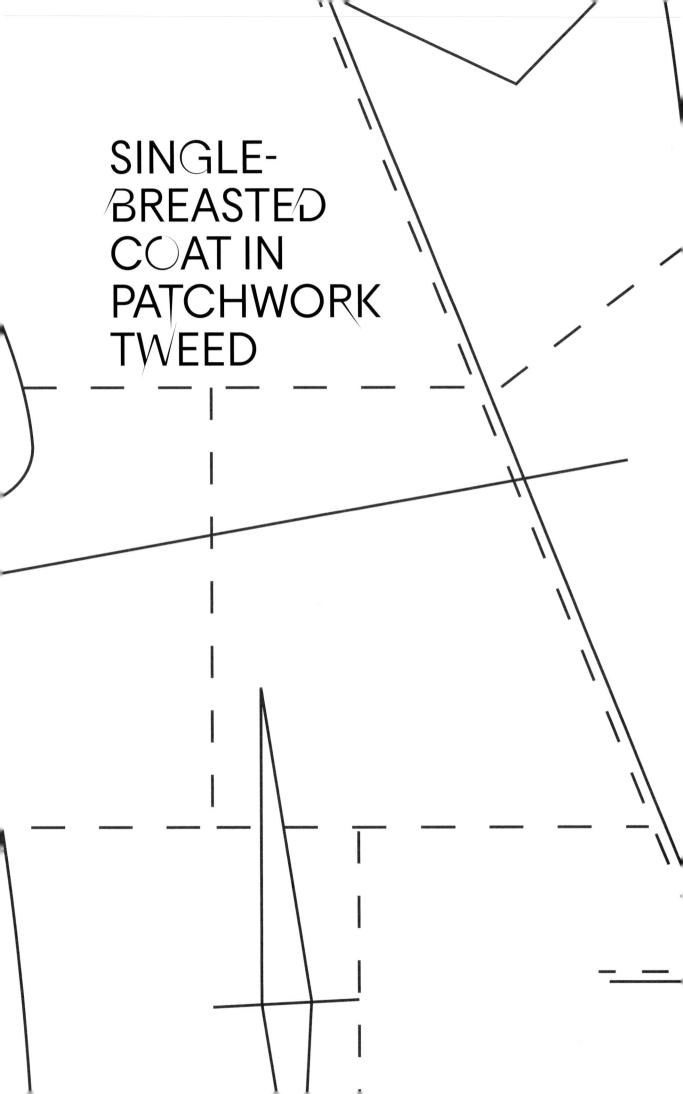

SINGLE-
BREASTED
COAT IN
PATCHWORK
TWEED

t was in June 2007 that Edward Wingler, an American theatre impresario and longtime customer carried over from my Huntsman days, came into No. 13 carrying a page torn out of a magazine. The page was an advertisement featuring a photograph of a young man in a patchwork-tweed jacket winding up to throw an American football.

'I'd like one of these,' he said, pointing to the coat.

Patchwork tweed, once a symbol of the Irish working class, has since achieved a new socioeconomic status due to its warmth, durability and evocation of old-world quality and charm. Mr Wingler's request, it seemed to me, warranted the very best tweeds around, which immediately put me in mind of Shetland, a tweed woven from sheep raised on the Shetland Islands north of mainland Scotland. Shetland tweed has its own special character: it is a rich, loose, porous, open wool, as opposed to a heavy, clean cut. As the *Gentleman's Gazette* succinctly put it, Shetland is 'the epitome of a casual tweed', and being in agreement I set about showing Mr Wingler some samples of it from W. Bill, an esteemed cloth manufacturer that has been selling some of the world's best Shetlands since 1846.

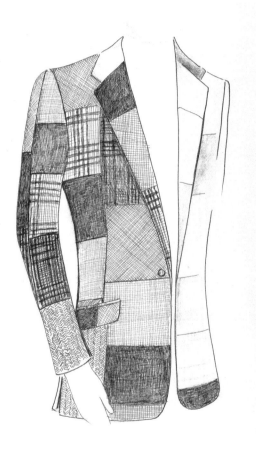

We settled on a nice medium weight of 12 ounces (340 grams), which breathes well and looks heavier than it actually is – a welcome advantage for anyone with a body temperature on the high side, or for achieving a classic woolly look well into spring or in early autumn. But even after deciding on a weight we still had 150 swatches to choose from. And there was another important question: how many different patches did we need? After some experimentation on a mood board – a kind of collage space that artists and designers use to get a flavour of how different aesthetic elements work together – I came to the conclusion that nine was the magic number. Nine different fabrics, in rectangles of approximately 5 by 6 centimetres each: this would give the coat a sufficiently motley look without overdoing it.

Once this had been decided, Mr Wingler and I considered a few different palettes. In his early seventies at the time, but still very much a dandy, Mr Wingler thought he would prefer something with a predominantly blue palette, while for contrast and curiosity's sake I decided simultaneously to make up a model of warm browns with splashes of red and grey. In the normal run of things, we need about 2 metres of cloth to make up a coat; for the patchwork ones we ordered 30 centimetres of each of the nine fabrics selected, for a total of 2.7 metres. Then I or one of my assistants cut up the nine fabrics into the 5 by 6 centimetre rectangles and these were machined together by one of our alteration tailors. A seam of about ⅜ to ½ inch was left around each of the patches' edges, for strength: this overage ensures that the seams hold together and don't 'grin', that is, stretch and pull apart. At my request the pieces were assembled in a mostly random order, avoiding putting two identical squares right next to each other;

this gives the coat a rough and ready look, versus an aspect that could feel overdetermined and too 'correct'.

Once the patches had been cut and sewn into this blanket of sorts, I then struck out the fabric in the usual way. Patched-together tweed, if done well, behaves just like whole cloth: there are no problems with getting it to lie flat or in achieving the customer's pattern. In addition to the regular-sized patches, the two slanted hip-pocket flaps and the outbreast pocket welt are also done in patched-together fabric, again selected to contrast with the surrounding material. The seamed underside of the material is of course eventually hidden by the coat's lining, typically an Ermazine in a muted colour that matches or complements the coat's base palette. Given how busy the outside is, you want to keep the inside simple.

Since finishing Mr Wingler's blueish version and putting our own warm-browns model in the window nearly ten years ago, we've taken orders for about twenty more patchwork coats. Like the denim suit (*see pages 76–81*), the patchwork coat has really hit a note with our under-35 customers – who, incidentally, make up only about 20% of our bespoke business (though more of the ready-to-wear), and yet this number is substantially higher than it would have been at Huntsman, where the average customer's age was 55-plus. The patchwork is also especially popular with my German clientele, maybe for reasons having to do with the fact that *Tweed Magazine*, a kind of fashion fanzine dedicated to 'the British way of life', is a German publication.

Each customer who has ordered one of our patchwork tweed coats has accepted the recommended quota of nine patches. However – and this is the fun part – choosing which nine is entirely down to the customer's taste

*Above: Our warm-browns model, styled by Barry Komen. Opposite:*
*Detail of the different Shetland tweeds (main image); and view of*
*'wrong side', showing how the patchwork is sewn together (inset).*

and whims. Most have gone with something similar to our single-breasted 'browns' model, though one of the aforementioned Germans, a financier, plumped for a double-breasted version in blues similar to Mr Wingler's. The writer Brian Masters, famous for his books on serial killers including Dennis Nilsen, Jeffrey Dahmer and Rosemary West, opted for a redder selection, including a bold crimson pocket welt and flaps. It looked fabulous, in my opinion, and apparently in his as well, given that shortly after picking it up he came back wanting a flat cap to match. Which we duly commissioned for him from none other than W. Bill.

*The coat is made from nine different Shetland tweeds and has a*
*3¼-inch notched lapel (above and opposite top), one-button fastening*
*(above) and angled pockets with flaps (above and opposite bottom).*

# SINGLE-BREASTED THREE-PIECE SUIT IN ITALIAN DONEGAL TWEED

Donegal tweed hails from County Donegal in Ireland's Ulster province, where sheep roam in the local hills and bogs; the material is coloured using dyes drawn from indigenous plants including blackberries, fuchsia, gorse and moss. In the late eighteenth century, the Royal Linen Manufacturers of Ulster reportedly distributed roughly six thousand looms and flax wheels to Donegal homesteads, encouraging the rise of the homespun tweed industry in the 1800s. Herringbone and check patterns are still commonly produced today – the cloth manufacturer W. Bill has been making them for more than 150 years – but the area is mostly known for its relatively heavy (15–16 ounces/425–455 grams) plain-weave wools with a base colour of lovat, brown or blue. Into

these base colours small bits of different-coloured yarn, or 'slubs', are woven to achieve a flecked effect that recalls the region's natural heathers and lichens. Regardless of its geographical origins, any fabric that has this flecked characteristic can be called 'donegal'.

A close relative to the true Irish Donegal fabric is Scottish thornproof donegal tweed. Thornproof tweed has a tighter, higher-twist weave that makes it less easily punctured by the thorns and branches that a wearer might encounter during shooting excursions. Porter & Harding, a fabric-maker founded in 1947 by John Porter and Bill Harding, themselves country sporting fans, is a company famous for producing Scottish thornproof donegal tweed. The fabric ranges from 12 to 18 ounces (340–510 grams) and, in the highest-quality versions, is a 'self-repairing' cloth, meaning that if it is pierced by a sharp object, simply massaging the point of puncture will make the resulting hole disappear. One of our regular clients, a Greek shipping magnate who wears almost only conservative blue and grey business suits, came in one day looking for a material that was a little harder-wearing than his usual worsted. When we showed him an 18-ounce (510-gram) Scottish thornproof donegal, he loved it, and wound up ordering two suits in navy and another two in grey. In addition to its durability, another reason Scottish donegal is often used for shooting suits is because its natural flecked appearance acts as a kind of camouflage.

The third most common type of donegal tweed is the Italian version. In recent years Italians have been combining traditional Irish Donegal and Scottish thornproof donegal to achieve a unique medium-weight fabric (10–11 ounces/285–310 grams) that has a softer handle than its Irish and Scottish counterparts and can be worn more or less nine months of the year. Italian donegal tweed has a base range of seven or eight colours and is typically used to make up sportcoats destined not for traipsing through the prickly underbrush but for, say, enjoying an *al fresco* aperitivo in the fashion quadrangle of Milan. When I worked at Huntsman, both Irish Donegal and Scottish donegal were extremely popular among customers wanting suits, overcoats or shooting clothes, including plus-twos and plus-fours – hunting breeches or knickerbockers that extend 2 or 4 inches below the knee, respectively (*see page 110*). The softer, lighter, more modern Italian donegal hadn't yet been conceived; when it finally was, we at Richard Anderson decided to use a beautiful pebble-coloured specimen to make

up this single-breasted three-piece suit. The fabric reminds me of the tweed suits men were always coming into Huntsman wearing on a Friday afternoon because of their versatility: you could wear Irish or Scottish donegal to the office during the day but also out to the countryside on a Friday night and feel equally comfortable in both milieus. In the same spirit, Italian donegal echoes the Irish and Scottish versions but also breathes new life into this classic aesthetic: somehow it looks and feels younger and fresher, yet the material is no less adaptable, as you can wear it to the office or even wear the jacket or waistcoat on its own, with jeans.

The three-piece suit dates back to at least the early 1900s, when the Victorian frock coat was replaced by sack coats and lounge coats, and three-piece ensembles consisted of a sack with a matching waistcoat or a vest often paired with contrasting trousers. It was also common at the time to wear a matching coat and trousers with a contrasting waistcoat. The waistcoat would typically fasten quite low and did not have a collar, whereas today one often sees waistcoats made to look somewhat more formal by the additional of a lapel. On our Italian donegal three-piece, for a slightly sportier look and feel, we added a lapel to the waistcoat and an outside ticket pocket to the coat. Otherwise, cutting a waistcoat essentially follows a customer's basic single-breasted coat pattern (*sans* sleeves of course), though with a slightly snugger fit achieved in accordance with the principles outlined on page 60.

During my early years at Huntsman, I became friends with one of the young tie salesmen who often came in: Robert Godley, then an employee of Drake's of London and now the founder and co-owner of Psycho Bunny,

*Above: Original fashion sketch showing options for our Italian donegal suit. Opposite: Close-up of the fabric, with its distinctive flecked appearance and softer handle.*

a hip clothing company that combines 'refined English tailoring with bold American design'. Robert has been our client at Richard Anderson for three years now, and he loves Italian donegal – because, I think, his background in exclusive fabrics has given him a great eye for new takes on old styles and, of course, an appreciation for Italian donegal's soft handle. He's ordered suits and jackets in at least four or five different Italian donegal fabrics, and often he'll wear the jacket on its own with a pair of Japanese-denim jeans (*see pages 76–81*). Italian donegal is also a favourite among our ready-to-wear customers, thanks to its sturdiness and faintly vintage aura. The material is informal, but still elegant enough to be worn on important business occasions, to a cocktail party, or even to a spring or autumn wedding in the Highlands – where its brightly coloured flecks will really come alive, glinting in the sun.

*Above: Edward Steichen portrait of American heavyweight boxing champion James Braddock wearing a donegal tweed three-piece suit,* Vanity Fair, *1924. Opposite: The single-breasted coat with slanted pockets and matching waistcoat with lapel.*

TWO-PIECE
SHOOTING
SUIT WITH
PLEATED BACK
IN LOVAT
THORNPROOF
TWEED

Prior to Victorian times, when shooting was taken up by the growing middle classes (along with tennis, golf, walking and cycling – all of which inspired fashionable clothing specific to such pursuits), men tended to shoot in whatever outdoor clothing came to hand: heavy garments made of broadcloth, worsted wool or fustian. The rise of Victorian railways made it possible for people to live and work in the city but travel regularly out to the country for sport, and shooting became a popular way to pass the time when visiting friends and family at their rural estates. After the Prince of Wales appeared in an all-tweed shooting suit in the 1860s, what one wore onto the grouse moor became more important still. Some say it was this royal intervention that gave rise to the supremely elegant tweed ensembles that shooting enthusiasts still wear today. While traditional shooting clothes have faced some competition in recent years from synthetic off-the-rack weatherproofed outerwear, only a bespoke coat will accommodate the wearer's arm movements ideally. Moreover, its seams stand a good chance of outlasting those on any cheaper machine-made, mass-produced garment.

Here at Richard Anderson we begin any shooting-suit consultation with the question: Are you actually intending to wear the suit shooting? The reason we ask is because if you do want to wear the suit shooting, then ideally – indeed, necessarily – the coat will have a pleat in the back. This allows the coat to expand when you raise your arms to take aim; then, when you lower your gun to see how you've done, the pleat closes. It's more challenging to include the pleat, which adds an extra four or five hours to the cutting and tailoring process, and some customers prefer a pleatless look. For this reason, many people who like the general style of a shooting coat but don't plan to shoot in it elect to do without the pleat. By the same token, many of my customers who don't intend to do any shooting opt to include a pleat nonetheless – for authenticity, I suppose, or perhaps in order to preserve the possibility of going shooting one day, should the opportunity ever arise.

Now: What fabric?

There are two chief criteria for choosing material for a shooting suit destined for actual shooting. The first is that you should consider fabrics that are warm, hard-wearing and perhaps even specially woven to resist

*The shooting coat is made in lovat thornproof tweed from Porter & Harding with a red-and-blue overcheck, fawn staghorn buttons and leather trim.*

puncture by thorns and brambles (*see page 103*). The colour and pattern are also important, because part of any serious shooter's technique is to blend in with the countryside that surrounds him. At Huntsman in the 1980s, we would annually select 30–40 different shades and overchecks designed specifically for rural sporting wear. We had a customer named M. R. Warren, a High Sheriff who every two or three years would come in to collect a 'blanket' like the one in the picture below – made up of two dozen or so different tweed samples – and take it home with him to his estate in Lewes, Sussex. There, he would drape it over a slope at the far end of his garden so that he could assess which pattern offered the best camouflage. Then it was up to us to turn the winning fabric into a shooting suit in time for the Glorious Twelfth, otherwise known as 12 August, the official start of grouse-shooting season.

*BUTTON 3 TWEED SHOOTING PATTERN*
*WITH PLEATED BACK*

The two-piece shooting suit here is made of a thornproof tweed in lovat with a red-and-blue overcheck. The material is from Porter & Harding and weighs 12–13 ounces (340–370 grams). The coat is a button-three, with buttons made of natural fawn staghorn, and has slanted pockets with a flap and an outside ticket pocket that have been trimmed with brown leather. It also has a leather gun patch on the right shoulder to protect the material underneath from the recurring friction of a gun's recoil.

Many shooting coats are paired with matching waistcoats and breeches called plus-twos or plus-fours, plus-twos being more common nowadays than plus-fours because they're slimmer and thus more stylish. Plus-twos have no pleats, a plain front, a narrower leg and a shorter overhang of 2 inches on the double, whereas plus-fours are much wider in the leg and have a 4-inch overhang on the double, which means they are roomier and offer more coverage (*see also page 104*). In this case, the client wanted ankle-length trousers, which we made with a wide 2-inch waistband and an adjustable strap. We also gave the trousers leather jettings on both the front and the back; these match the trim on the coat. The cut of the legs is narrow enough that at the bottom they can be tucked into socks or boots – a useful option on wet or muddy terrain. The suit's lining is a plain matching Ermazine. Finally, we've equipped the coat with what's known as a poacher's pocket, primarily for gun cartridges but historically used for stealing all manner of items on and off the Highlands.

*Above: Pattern illustration showing forepart, side-body pleated back and sleeve.*

*Above: The coat has a suede gun patch to the right shoulder (top), a
3-inch notched lapel, leather welt outbreast pocket and ¼-inch swelled
edges to lapel with a 1-inch hand-worked lapel hole (inset).*

*Caricature by 'Spy' of the Earl de Grey, then the best game shot in England, wearing a similar lovat tweed shooting suit with plus-fours, Vanity Fair, 1890.*

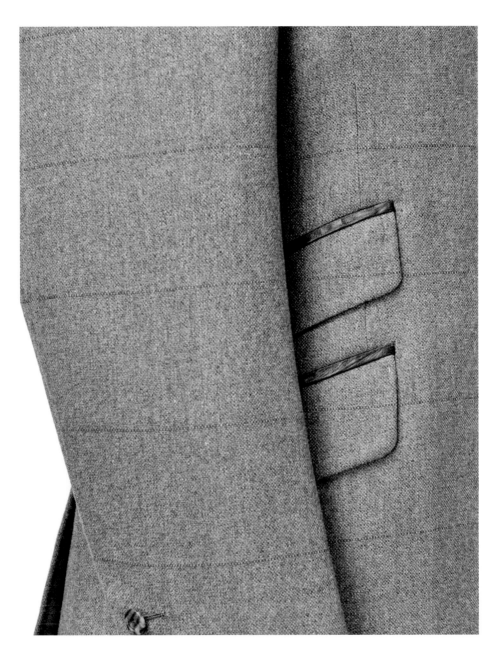

A large interior pocket in which a shooter might hide a felled partridge or hare, a poacher's pocket is prevented from visibly weighing down the coat by a strip of fabric that suspends the pocket in place. Like shooting suits themselves, the practice of smuggling one's conquests home from the field is so evocative of British tradition that 'The Poacher's Pocket' is now a common name for country pubs. One English poacher has even become legendary for his vocation: Jim Hawker, from Daventry, Northamptonshire, whose headstone is said to have read: 'I will Poach till I die.' Judging from the twenty or so shooting suit orders I continue to receive each year, it seems this is how many men feel about shooting itself.

*The slanted exterior pockets are trimmed with ¼-inch leather jetting; inside the coat is a concealed poacher's pocket.*

# SINGLE-
# BREASTED
# COAT IN
# ARDALANISH
# PEBBLE
# DIAMOND
# TWILL

M any of Richard Anderson Ltd's customers are not merely clotheshorses but moonlight in fashion design as well. One such client is Carlton Browne, of Newport Beach, California, who came recommended to my business partner, Brian Lishak, by an old Huntsman customer and friend. Mr Browne rarely misses an opportunity to meet up with Brian when Brian pays his three annual visits to the Beverly Wilshire Hotel, and so it happened that in January 2012 he showed up with a box of samples that he had sourced from a company called A. A. Smith. This was a modest Scottish wool mill recently purchased by Andrew and Anne Smith, and Brian was genuinely impressed by the cloths, some of which were retro designs he hadn't seen in 50 years or

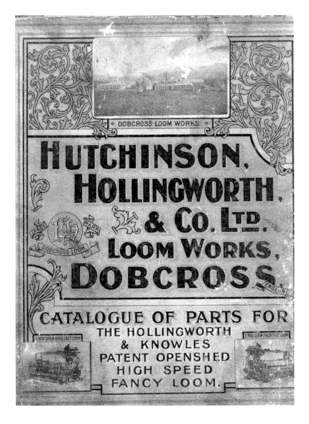

more. Achieved with mainly natural dyes, the designs included fine herringbones, diamond twills, checks and stripes, and heavy diagonal weaves unique and indeed very distinct from those available from our usual tweed suppliers. The material's look, manufacturing method and handle – it's extremely dry, which is to say not scratchy or hairy, like a Harris tweed, but soft without being overly silky – impressed Brian so much that he agreed on the spot to make it up into a coat for Mr Browne, who also graciously donated his box of samples for the benefit of future customers' inspiration.

Ardalanish refers to what was formerly a village on the Scottish Isle of Mull in Argyll and Bute, but which is now the Smiths' organic farm and weaving mill: Ardalanish, Isle of Mull Weavers. Ardalanish wool – which comes from the Hebridean sheep raised on the farm, as well as from other native varieties of sheep from farms in the vicinity, including Shetland and Manx Loaghtan – weighs in at about 17 ounces (480 grams). The natural colour of the wool produced by the animals varies from year to year, yielding shades from black and charcoal brown to fawn, silvery greys and creamy whites. Plant dyes including woad and madder are also used, but even so the fabrics' hues rarely deviate from nature's own muted tones, with the occasional hint of a sky blue or rose pink. The mill uses Victorian Dobcross power looms, which are said to have helped sustain Britain's textile industry for more than a century: although slower than modern looms, they afford the weaver much greater control and oversight of every inch of material produced.

As mentioned, the Smiths issue their samples in a box, rather than in a bunch or book like most other suppliers, and even before the fabled

*Catalogue of parts, c. 1898, for the Victorian Dobcross power looms still used by the Ardalanish weaving mill.*

container arrived at No. 13 Savile Row, customer after customer had pored over it and dreamed up a look. One was the Reverend Richard (Dick) Fabian, another longtime customer and friend, who, in San Francisco, Brian's first port of call after LA, liked the material enough to order three single-breasted sportcoats in it – in Natural Diamond Twill, Mull Granite and Silver Keystone – right on the spot. Also won over was our friend the American poet Fred Seidel, who chose a silver pheasant-eye spot – a sort of birdseye pattern, but larger – in which he wanted a duplicate of a riding coat my old Huntsman mentor Brian Hall had made for him many times. The pattern has two high buttons in the front and one deep vent in the back, to accommodate the normal horseback-riding stance (or, in Fred's case, the Ducati-riding stance). At Huntsman there was actually an old saddle in which customers sat in order to be fitted in riding coats. Here at Richard Anderson we make do with a simple chair facing backward: the customer sits on it and leans forward slightly, as if to pull tightly on the reins of a horse or grip the handlebars of a bike. Accordingly, you have to cut the back a little wider,

*Above: Close-up texture of the beautiful Ardalanish fabric in a light grey-and-white pebble diamond twill. Opposite: The coat is single-breasted, with a two-button front and slanted pockets with flaps.*

adding ¼ inch to either side; you also have to pitch the sleeves forward slightly and give a bit of extra material through the hind arm of each sleeve. These are only subtle differences, hardly noticeable, if at all, when the customer is walking, standing or sitting in the usual way, but they can make all the difference when the coat is used for its designated purpose, which is to say hunkering down and going fast.

Other than Mr Seidel's riding coat, only one of the Ardalanish coats we've made thus far has been double-breasted: a light grey-and-white pebble diamond twill, which the eminent William Gilchrist, stylist to Jude Law and the Rolling Stones, decided to have made into a three-piece suit. The portrait painter Luke Haseler (whose uncanny likenesses of Brian and

myself hang watchfully over the shop) also chose a pebble diamond twill for a coat and trousers set. We've made several overcoats, too, with the material, given its warmth, and when its popularity became too rampant to ignore we went ahead and ordered 30 metres of it for our ready-to-wear line.

Aside from its inherent qualities – its durability, its luxurious but not extravagant feel and its exquisite look – I love Ardalanish wool perhaps most of all for the simple reason that my esteemed Huntsman tutors would have loved it, too. It's heavy, but not too heavy. It has historical significance and integrity. Huntsman was renowned for its colourful tweeds, especially in bold designs; they were made by a manufacturer called T. M. Hunter, of Brora in mainland Scotland, which, like Ardalanish, used old-fashioned looms not only to produce fabric for clothing but also blankets with various colourways highlighting their warp and weft. With its old-fashioned patterns, especially stripes (rare on a tweed), Ardalanish also reminds me of the fabric Huntsman's tweed aficionado Mr Packer and his wife used to select for their famous his-and-hers matching three-piece suits. So Ardalanish has something of the old Huntsman glory to it – and yet it's also very much Richard Anderson's own. Versatile, visually hip and environmentally conscious, it is at once tantalizingly vintage *and* of the twenty-first century.

*Above: Stylist William Gilchrist wearing his three-piece double-breasted suit made from Ardalanish pebble diamond twill.*

*Top: The coat has a 3¼-inch notched lapel and three-button cuffs. Inset: Pattern illustration showing forepart and side-body of Fred Seidel's high two-button riding coat.*

119

# TOP COATS

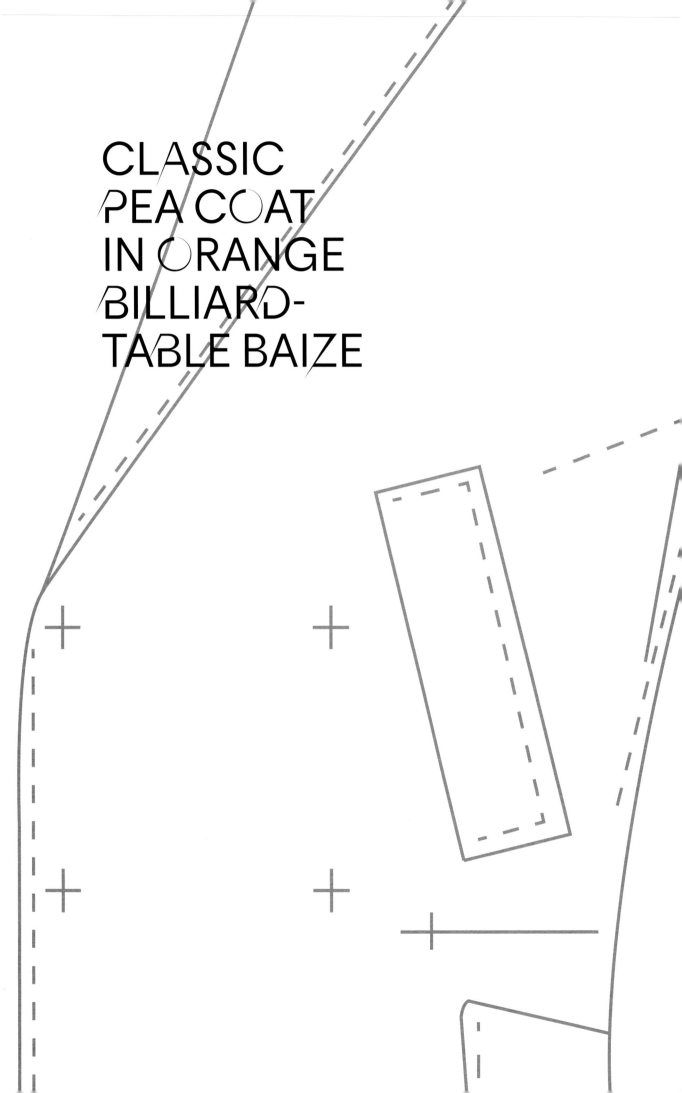

CLASSIC
PEA COAT
IN ORANGE
BILLIARD-
TABLE BAIZE

I have read two theories on the origin of the term 'pea coat': one comes from the *Mariner's Mirror*, the quarterly journal of the British Society for Nautical Research, which suggests it derives from the Dutch or West Frisian word *pijjekker*, or *pijjakker* – *pij* referring to the type of cloth used for British and later American sailors' coats: a coarse blue twill with a nap on one side. The other theory, offered up by the *Origin of Navy Terminology*, suggests that the heavy material used to make such rugged seafaring outerwear was referred to as 'pilot cloth', shortened to 'P-cloth', and thus

the resulting garment became a 'P-jacket', or 'P-coat'. Whatever its etymology, the classic pea coat was a staple at Huntsman, where my esteemed teacher Colin Hammick made at least three different versions of it for the Duke of Beaufort and Gianni Agnelli (each); Hammick was also responsible for the one a windswept Gregory Peck is wearing as he squints manfully out to sea in a famous photo still from the movie adaptation of *Moby Dick* (1956). But when I say 'different versions' I mean in texture or weight only; almost always, Hammick's iconic pea coat had six buttons down the front, a standard outbreast pocket on top and jetted flapless ones below, a regular peaked lapel, and – most importantly – it was navy blue. A colour so-called, of course, because it was the standard colour of the British naval uniform.

A few years into the present century, however, the pea coat as we knew it seemed to me due for a little revamping. And what better way to get a classic model noticed again than reconceiving it in a bold new colour? Unfortunately, material in the exact hue I had in mind – shocking orange, which is directly opposite classic navy on the colour wheel – is something of a rare commodity. I had seen it before only on the surface of pool tables, where it is perhaps the most popular alternative to the verdant green meant to evoke the lawn games from which billiards evolved. And so I duly tracked the material down through Hainsworth, a small cloth supplier we deal with that happens also to source the material for billiard surfaces: a woven wool or wool-nylon blend called baize, whose variations in weight and nap, incidentally, can have a crucial effect on the speed and 'swerve' of a pool or snooker ball.

The orange baize we used for our ultramodern pea coat comes from the Spring Valley Mill in West Yorkshire and is rather lighter than the material

*The classic double-breasted pea coat, 'button three show three', reimagined in a bold, modern orange baize with black livery buttons.*

typically selected to keep boatswains and whalers warm. This matter of weight is relevant not only to a garment's functionality but also to the cutter's job. With heavier material, it is easier to cut a crisp and distinct line, because the material more readily and lastingly holds the shape the cutter gives it. Hammick and Hall would have been aghast at the prospect of cutting a coat in material that was only 7½ ounces (210 grams); 13 ounces (370 grams) was 'lightweight' to them. But over the last quarter-century or so things have changed. Most of us now enjoy central heating, whereas a good number of Huntsman's customers lived in draughty old townhouses or, for that matter, castles. And with global warming, the need for very heavy

outerwear, or indeed innerwear, has waned. This gives a cutter like myself more flexibility to be creative with a wider range of weights and textures; however, it also demands more skill in the cutting room, where working with a cloth that weighs as much as 20–25 ounces (570–710 grams) can give you, shall we say, a head start. These days, one would typically make a pea coat in heavy navy serge (22 ounces/ 625 grams), a woolen cashmere blend (18 ounces/510 grams), a heavy gabardine (16–18 ounces/455–510 grams), doeskin (20 ounces/570 grams), or a cavalry twill Merino wool (24 ounces/680 grams). By contrast, the West Country billiards-table baize I'd ordered is significantly lighter than these usual suspects: about 11 ounces (310 grams), which is to say lighter than every one of the fabrics Hammick or Hall would have recommended pre-1985 to a customer in the market for a 'summer' suit.

Modern fashion has got hold of the pea coat, which means that these days you can find plenty of variations. As far as the cut itself is concerned, however, I typically stick to the classic lines. This is short – 1½ or 2 inches longer than the customer's regular suit jacket – with a double-breasted front, six large buttons, a deep collar and wide lapels. Unlike overcoats, which have a single vent in the back, a pea coat typically has two vents, each 7–8 inches long, and two welted pockets cut horizontally across the front (welted meaning, essentially, 'without a flap'). The only significant tweaks I've done to the classic style – other than its colour, of course – is to make it slightly more fitted, and to add a second pair of pockets. In addition to the standard horizontal welted pockets, my model has vertical ones on either side, giving the wearer the option of lodging his hands in this lower, slightly more casual, position.

*Original fashion sketch showing options considered for lapel shapes, and horizontal and vertical slant welted pockets.*

*Gregory Peck wearing a pea coat made by my mentor Colin Hammick
in the film* Moby Dick *(1956).*

*As the orange baize, from Spring Valley Mill in West Yorkshire, is of a
lighter weight than the very heavy wool traditionally used for pea coats,
it requires especially skilled cutting to produce the same crisp lines.*

Shortly after I'd ordered up the orange baize for our new pea coat and made a model for our window, *Esquire* caught wind of it and ran a photo in its March 2004 fashion special. The result? People started coming into the shop eager to order a pea coat – but everyone wanted one in blue! This happens, and with amusing regularity: you reconceive a classic in a specialist colour or material in order to revive its popularity and instead you spark a renaissance of interest in the original version. In fact I think I've made only one orange pea coat to order, in addition to the model. I did do one in British racing green, but all of the rest have been in good old navy. There was one memorable deviation from the norm, when soon after taking home his finished pea coat a customer happened to see *Three Days of the Condor* (1975), in which Robert Redford wears one with a collar so large that when he flips it upward his head all but disappears. The customer came back and wanted a 'Robert Redford collar', which I happily swapped in for him.

*Robert Redford wearing a pea coat with oversized, turned-up collar in the film* Three Days of the Condor *(1975).*

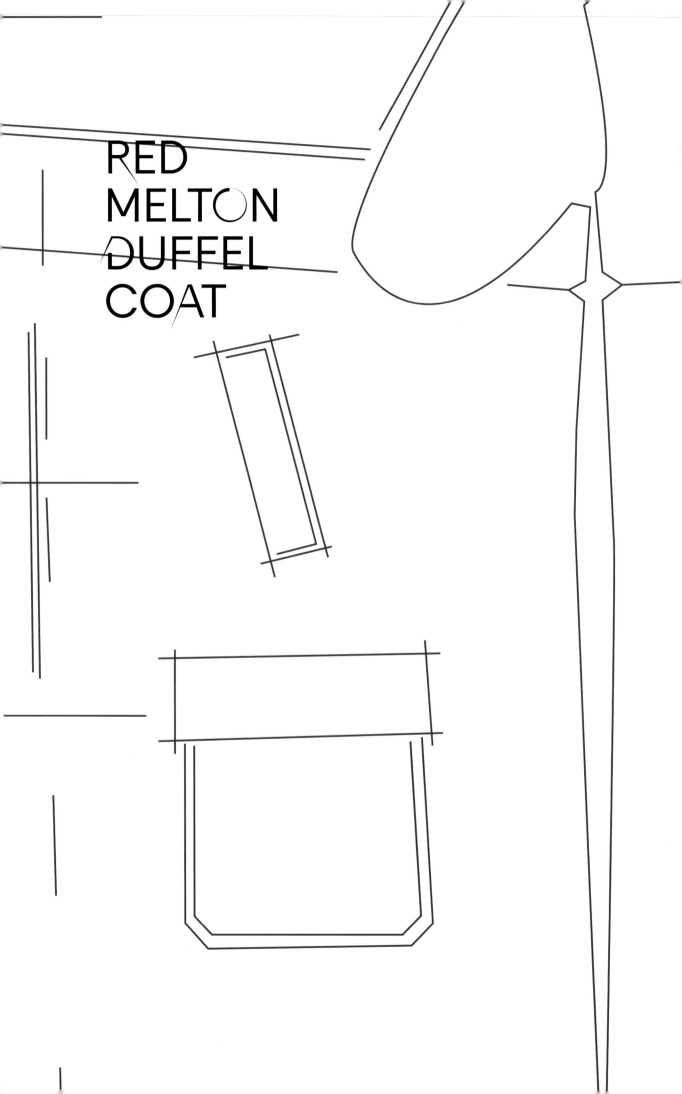

RED
MELTON
DUFFEL
COAT

The duffel or 'duffle' coat takes its name from the small town of Duffel, in the Antwerp province of Belgium, from which the thick woollen material originally used to make duffel coats and bags hails. There are many variations on the duffel coat, but typically the original British style would be knee-length or shorter and made of a genuine double-weave duffel, with three or four toggles in wood or horn running down the front and fastened by a short piece of leather or rope. It would also have two large patch pockets on the outside and a roomy 'bucket' hood, which in more modern models would occasionally be substituted

with what's called a 'pancake' hood, because it's rounder and flatter and so resembles a pancake lying against the back. The duffel coat has long been popular with people in extreme-weather lines of work, including policemen and military personnel, because its fabric is heavy and warm, the toggles are easily fastenable by fingers wearing gloves and the hood fits easily over a uniform cap. Indeed, the coat was being supplied to servicemen in the British Royal Navy as early as 1890, and both Winston Churchill and Field Marshal Montgomery can be seen wearing a duffel coat in numerous photographic portraits taken during and after the Second World War. Montgomery is said to have been so fond of the duffel coat that his troops eventually nicknamed it 'the Monty coat'.

In the late 1940s, '50s and '60s, the duffel coat gained widespread appeal and began to appear prominently in popular culture as well. Trevor Howard, playing Major Calloway, wears a duffel coat in almost every one of his scenes in *The Third Man* (1949). A blue two-toggle model is the famous uniform of Paddington Bear. Jean Cocteau wore a short white version while strolling in Rome with Coco Chanel, and, more recently, the Glaswegian band Belle and Sebastian and the members of Oasis have all been seen in duffel coats, Oasis on the cover of their single 'Roll with It'. But the duffel coat was very rarely, if ever, a style seen on Savile Row – not until 2001, when I received a phone call from a German customer by the name of Carl Krautwig, who'd been referred to us by the bespoke shirtmaker Sean O'Flynn. This was back when I had recently left Huntsman but not yet opened up my own shop, yet the undaunted Mr Krautwig nonetheless ordered two suits and a blazer from me straightaway. Once we did have a shop, he began to come in with ever-more creative ideas, including the request that I make him something he had wanted for some time: a bespoke duffel coat.

*Mannequin shot of the red melton duffel coat showing four-toggle front, bucket hood and patch pockets with flaps.*

Had my old mentors Colin Hammick or Brian Hall been on the receiving end of such a request, the customer very likely would have been laughed right off the Row. But at fledgling Richard Anderson we were in no position to turn down business, so I took the suggestion on, and I'm glad I did.

While original duffel coats were, as mentioned, typically made of duffel, nowadays they tend to be made of melton, which is a somewhat softer, napped wool whose name comes from the Leicestershire town of Melton Mowbray. Mr Krautwig wanted his duffel coat in red melton, which we ordered from Dormeuil: a relatively heavy 20-ounce (565-gram) material that, like duffel itself, is warm, durable and resistant to harsh weather. Having never made a duffel coat before, I was prepared for a process that involved a bit of trial and error. Not wanting to waste any of our exquisite Dormeuil melton, I initially struck out a toile of the coat in some leftover tweed. This was especially helpful in terms of getting the proportions of the bucket hood right. To the outside of the coat, we added two large patch pockets, each with a flap. We straightened the side seams slightly and cut the coat without a centre-back seam, which is to say we gave it a yoke (*see page 133*); this results in a less fitted silhouette than that of a typical Richard Anderson coat – after all, a duffel coat might be worn over a suit, bulky jumper or blazer. The yoke also serves to encourage rain and snowmelt to run right off the coat's back. Another cutting consideration specific to the duffel coat is that to accommodate the toggles one must add an extra ½ inch to the coat's front edge.

Once the tweed baste version was ready, we had a fitting with Mr Krautwig, who approved of the pattern, giving us the green light to proceed with the crimson melton itself. As ever in a proper bespoke garment, the coat was

*Field Marshal Bernard Montgomery (1887–1976) in 1946, wearing his signature duffel coat, which British soldiers during the Second World War nicknamed the 'Monty coat'.*

*Our duffel coat is made of an exquisitely soft, yet heavy and warm, red melton fabric from Dormeuil, with double machine-stitching to front yoke, pockets and front edge.*

131

completely hand-canvassed, but because of the weight and structure of the material, integral to the coat's style, we elected also to double machine-stitch the edges to ensure they'd hold, a technique I learned at Huntsman many years ago. Our in-house tailors also hand-sewed the staghorn toggles and their leather fasteners onto the coat's front, and for its lining we used a matching red twill. We were so pleased with the final result that we asked Mr Krautwig if we might put his coat on display in our window for a while before he took possession of it, and he graciously obliged. We also featured the coat in our newsletter of late 2002/early 2003, and very soon were asked to make two more, both in blue: one in a navy twill for a New York banker, the other in a lightweight Bedford cord. This second one, fittingly enough, was for a man from the motherland of duffel's namesake: Belgium.

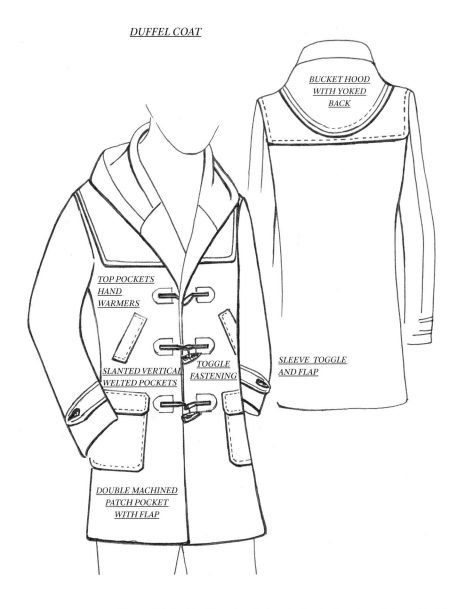

*DUFFEL COAT*

*BUCKET HOOD WITH YOKED BACK*

*TOP POCKETS HAND WARMERS*

*SLANTED VERTICAL WELTED POCKETS*

*TOGGLE FASTENING*

*SLEEVE TOGGLE AND FLAP*

*DOUBLE MACHINED PATCH POCKET WITH FLAP*

*Above: Original fashion sketch showing bucket hood, pockets and toggle front. Opposite: Details of staghorn toggles with leather loops.*

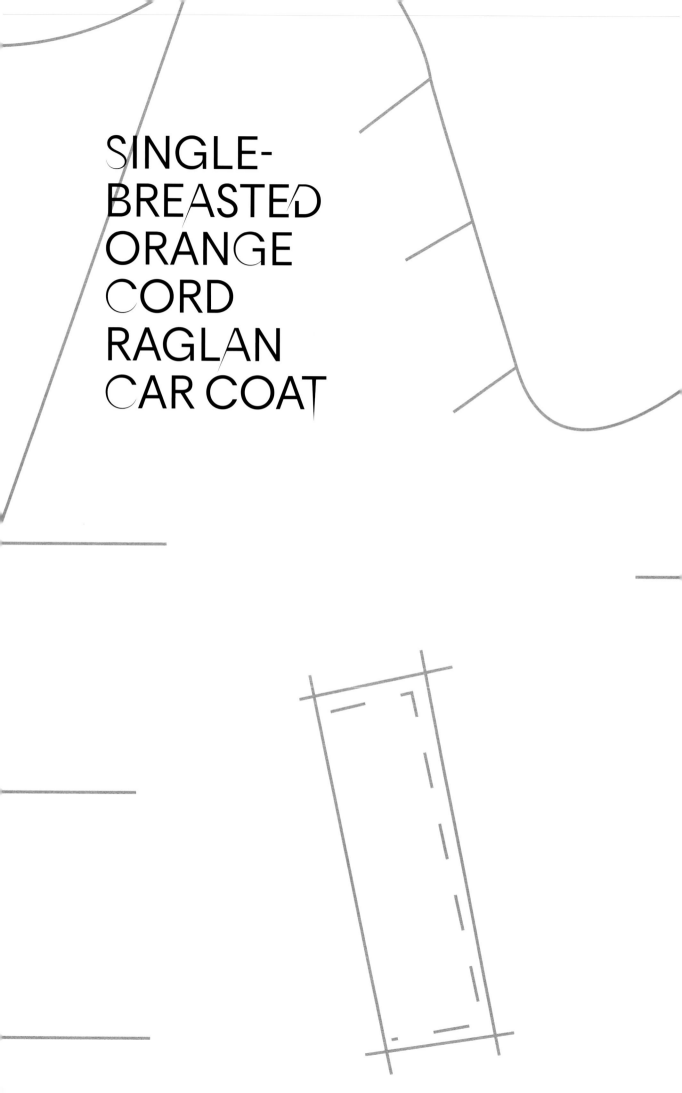

SINGLE-
BREASTED
ORANGE
CORD
RAGLAN
CAR COAT

W e owe the raglan sleeve (and much else, for that matter) to British Field Marshal Fitzroy James Henry Somerset, a.k.a. 1st Baron Raglan (1788–1855), commander of British forces during the Crimean War. Baron Raglan famously lost his right arm during the Battle of Waterloo (and then, according to legend, asked for it back, in order to retrieve a ring his wife had given him), and thereafter wore what became known as a 'raglan sleeve' to accommodate his stump. A raglan sleeve's seams slant outward from neck to underarm, dispensing

with the vertical shoulder seam on a 'normal' jacket and allowing for more freedom of movement (or, in Baron Raglan's case, an easier dressing experience). The raglan sleeve also yields a more rounded, sloping and casual look that has since become popular not only only on jackets, coats, blouses and dresses, but also on sweatshirts and t-shirts – whether short-sleeved, three-quarter-length, or long – including the two-toned garments worn by American baseball players under their uniforms, and sometimes even the baseball uniforms themselves.

When I started at Huntsman in the early 1980s, orders for raglan coats had begun to decline. But in the early half of the twentieth century the raglan style had been hugely popular and cut primarily by Hammick and Hall's own mentor and boss: a superlative Huntsman tailor named Cecil Pressland. In the 1960s and '70s, after 'Prez' had retired, if Hammick or Hall had a raglan order they would often elect to give it to an outside tailor to make up. This was in part because creating raglan sleeves requires an especially skilled hand, but also, I think, because the soft line of the style was antithetical to the crisper, more defined Huntsman silhouette that Hammick and Hall preferred. Indeed, they took on raglan orders only reluctantly, which perhaps encouraged the decline in raglan sales – in my opinion, a shame. In the mid-1990s, when I'd gained sufficient clout to speak my mind, I suggested that we launch a promotion featuring a raglan car coat in Huntsman's house check tweed. Right away, Huntsman took orders from a good many customers who

*Baron Raglan in a portrait* c. *1840, after losing an arm during the Crimean War; he popularized the eponymous raglan sleeve, which made it easier for him to dress.*

saw the model in our window on their way in. And thus, bespoke raglan was back.

Originally referred to as 'motoring dress', the car coat came into fashion in the early 1900s, when most cars were open-top and driving them required a protective garment for spruceness and warmth. Back then, car coats were typically long, and those worn in winter would be made of fur or have a fur lining. Summertime motoring dress was often referred to as a 'duster' or 'dust' coat, designed as it was to protect one's finer clothing from airborne particles. Commonly it would be made of a lightweight material such as linen or alpaca, the better to stay cool under direct sun. Motoring clothes gave rise to an accessory craze as well: gloves, goggles, hats and veils revved into fashion and were often worn off-road and year-round as well. By the 1950s, motoring dress had become shorter, modelled to an extent on the 'jeep coat' worn by military servicemen during the Second World War, and it came in many different fabrics of varying stain- and weather-resistance, including nylon, roebuck suede and poplin. Some designs featured toggle fastenings and detachable hoods that echoed their owners' convertibles. By the 1960s, the car coat was no longer merely for driving but was considered an official staple of any man's wardrobe. As John Taylor, editor of the *Tailor and Cutter* magazine, wrote in 1966: 'The riding mac was the equivalent in the 1920s and '30s of the car coat of the 1950s and '60s. If a riding mac was worn there was the suggestion that it had been bought for a specific purpose. The wearer probably owned a hack and therefore was not a member of the *hoi polloi*. For similar reasons today, however submerged in the psyches of their owners the reasons may lie, there are far more car coats in male wardrobes than there are cars in garages.'

Today, the car coat is typically a short, square-cut garment that's easy to throw on over a jacket or jumper. Accordingly, combining it with the loose-fitting raglan sleeve seemed an obvious union. As I've said, creating a raglan sleeve is something of a specialist skill, and to do it here at Richard Anderson we employ the estimable Carmelo Reina, who has worked on Savile Row for nearly 40 years. First it's up to me to convert the customer's standard lounge-coat pattern by adjusting the shoulders and length and straightening the side seams. Then Carmelo sews in the sleeves completely by hand, and with all the usual canvas for support and form. Usually

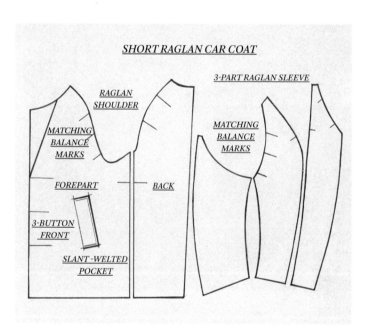

SHORT RAGLAN CAR COAT

3-PART RAGLAN SLEEVE

RAGLAN SHOULDER

MATCHING BALANCE MARKS

MATCHING BALANCE MARKS

FOREPART

BACK

3-BUTTON FRONT

SLANT-WELTED POCKET

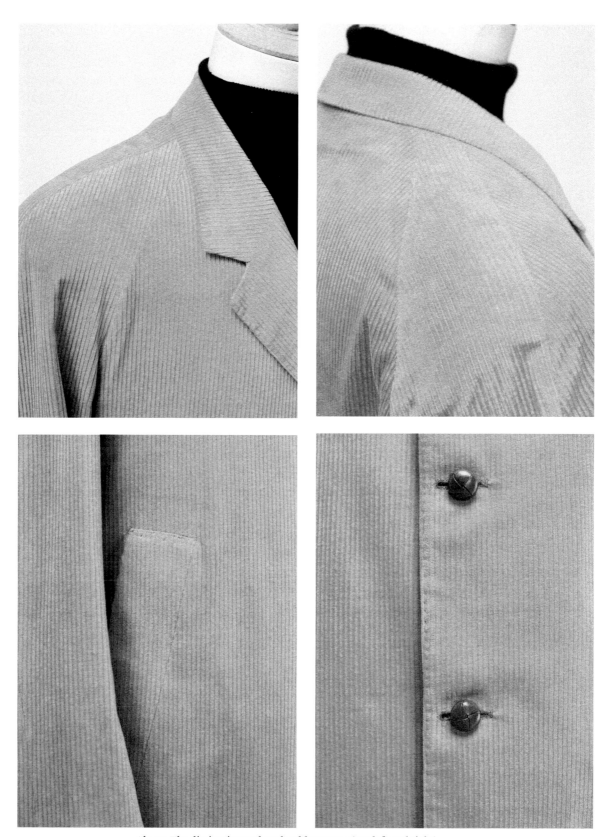

*Above: The distinctive raglan shoulder seams (top left and right);
vertical slanted 'hand warmer' pocket (bottom left) and antique leather
'football buttons' (bottom right). Opposite: Original fashion sketch
showing forepart, back and three-part raglan sleeves.*

a raglan coat is made up in tweed, but wanting to lighten the look a bit I experimented with making one in the cotton-cashmere orange corduroy from Scabal that you see here. We married it with a burgundy Ermazine lining and gave it leather football buttons, which resemble the antique brown-leather orbs premodern footballers used to kick around. Since then I've also made a woman's version, with slightly narrower shoulders, for the writer Jeanette Winterson, and another raglan car coat in blue corduroy for an art dealer who lives in Holland Park. We've also made a stone-coloured raglan raincoat in water-resistant gabardine for the architect I. M. Pei. Mr Pei wanted his made with a little extra flair around the bottom, a shape rather reminiscent of the pyramid he designed to sit outside the Louvre.

*Above: American baseball legend Lou Gehrig in his New York Yankees uniform with raglan sleeves. Opposite: Raglan car coats are normally made in tweed, but we used an orange cotton-cashmere corduroy from Scabal for an updated, lightweight version.*

# CLASSIC BOMBER JACKET IN IRISH DONEGAL TWEED

I n 2005, a longtime American customer of ours in his mid-fifties or so asked Brian, during one of Brian's regular visits to San Francisco, whether we would consider making him a bespoke bomber jacket. Initially, I was reluctant – my old Huntsman mentors wouldn't have touched such a request with a barge pole – but when the customer brought it up a second time and then a third we finally relented. He'd already chosen the fabric: an exquisite walnut-coloured Irish Donegal thornproof tweed (*see pages 102–7*) from Porter & Harding. And this was the reason he was so insistent we give the commission a try: you can buy a bomber jacket off the rack for a fraction of what it would cost on Savile Row; what's more, a bomber jacket can be moulded to the body only so much before it ceases to become a bomber jacket, which by definition is loose-fitting. But if you have your heart set on a specific style in a specific material and you can't find the combination elsewhere, your only choices are to make it yourself or bring it to your tailor and hope for the best.

One of the reasons I gave in is that this customer is the son of another longtime Huntsman customer, a US Navy admiral with whom we've enjoyed a long and congenial relationship. Colin Hammick cut for the admiral at Huntsman, and then I inherited him after our beloved Hammick died. A great lover of large-check three-piece suits and pocket watches, this man bequeathed to us as clients not only his son but also his grandson, making for three generations (and counting) of loyal patronage. So we have come to know the family well, which is why I felt reasonably confident that if our foray into bomber-jacket territory didn't work out, there was unikely to be any bad feeling because of it.

The bomber jacket – also known as a flight jacket, or bombardier jacket – was first created in the early twentieth century for use by First World War military pilots, whose cockpits were exposed. Typically made of heavy-duty leather and lined or partially lined with fur, the bomber jacket featured large fold-up or wraparound collars, zip closures with wind flaps, and close-fitting cuffs and waists, all designed to keep the wearer warm. Various models including the classic RAF sheepskin-lined flight jacket and the A-1 and A-2 jackets adopted by the US Army Air Corps (later the US Air Force) eventually gave way to lighter cloth-shell jackets like the cotton and nylon B-15s, as well as one of the first bomber jackets to feature a smaller, stand-up collar: the MA-1. By this time, the United States was at war in Vietnam, and, popular

*Original fashion sketch for our classic bomber jacket showing zip-front and a different style of elasticated collar and waistband.*

141

opposition to the conflict notwithstanding, civilian offshoots of the MA-1 bomber jacket became popular both in the States and abroad. Versions including baseball-style jackets with contrasting sleeves began popping up in London's mod scene, as well as on skinheads and scooterboys. Indeed, another reason I warmed to this most unusual commission is that I myself have considerable affection for a cousin of the bomber jacket: the Harrington jacket, which every last one of my friends and I wore to school in the 1980s. First introduced by Baracuta & Grenfell in the 1930s and nicknamed the 'Harrington jacket' because Ryan O'Neal donned a Baracuta G9 while playing Rodney Harrington in the television programme *Peyton Place* (1964–69), the Harrington jacket is essentially a lighter-weight version of the bomber jacket in cotton, wool, nylon, polyester or thin leather. It also has what we call a yoke, or a back seam, angled like an umbrella to encourage rain to run off the wearer's shoulders, and a distinctive tartan lining. It might as well have been my school's uniform.

*Second World War RAF pilots from Bomber Command wearing the classic early sheepskin-lined bomber jacket.*

*Our modern bespoke bomber jacket in walnut-coloured Irish Donegal thornproof tweed from Porter & Harding.*

*Above: Classic bomber-jacket details include the stand collar and heavy-duty front zip (top); and slant welted pockets and 2 inches of elasticated wool jersey to cuffs and waistband (inset).*

This tweed bomber jacket – or Harrington jacket, if you prefer – has a square front, slanted welted pockets on the outside, two pockets on the inside and an upright collar. The back is made of two pieces that come together in an inverted pleat and, at the top, the aforementioned yoke. There are two underarm darts, one on each side, to give a modicum of shape, plus sixteen small darts around the bottom of the jacket and a few more above each cuff, to make the fabric gather in at the elasticated bands of wool jersey. To cut the jacket I had to create a new pattern from scratch, but I was able to do this with the measurements we'd already recorded for the customer in question, who'd already ordered various suits and sportcoats from us and not gained or lost any significant weight. For the lining we used a cotton shirting in a 'hunt brown' tattersall check from a company called Acorn, and, indeed, it's much like the gingham check typically used to line hunt coats (*see page 176*). In this case we used the tattersall only for the body of the coat and gave the sleeves a plain Ermazine lining to reduce friction when the customer inserts and withdraws his arms. Finally, the jacket has a heavy, 24-inch metal zip – a feature that the bomber jackets of the First World War popularized for the first time. That something so commonplace was a novelty less than a century ago seems unfathomable now, when we throw on such a jacket, zip it up, and, without thinking, head out the door.

*Above: A group of RAF bomber pilots and flight maintenance staff in 1941; only pilots wore the bomber jacket as part of their uniform, adding to its cachet.*

DOUBLE-
BREASTED
LARGE BLACK-
AND-WHITE
PRINCE OF
WALES CHECK
OVERCOAT

It isn't easy to get through life without an overcoat. While it's rare for a brand-new customer to come in wanting an overcoat as his very first Savile Row garment, at least 40% of our regular customers have ordered a bespoke overcoat at some point in their patronage. (One man who lives in Ontario has had almost as many overcoats made as suits.) The most popular choices of overcoat fabric include cashmere, vicuña and tweed, with a median weight range of 18–22 ounces (510–625 grams) – though we've also made overcoats with material as light as 14–15 ounces (400–425 grams) and as heavy as 25–26 ounces (710–735 grams). My own overcoat of choice is the covert coat, so-named for its colour, which ranges from the brown or fawn to tannish-green of any thicket or other hiding place for game or animals in the wild. Originally designed for hunting and horseback riding, the covert coat, which is all wool but occasionally features a velvet collar, has evolved over the last century to become a generally lighter garment worn by a great many gentlemen today. This is because it's durable, comfortable, classic and drizzle-resistant; it's also, thanks to its neutral colour, widely versatile. It can be worn over practically any kind of ensemble, from a grey suit to a coral sportcoat to a t-shirt and jeans.

To create an overcoat pattern, one must amend the master pattern already created for the customer's lounge coat. On the back and at the top of the forepart one must add ⅞ inch; on the front edge, if converting from a single-breasted pattern to a single-breasted coat, you add 1¼ inch. Then, at each of the side seams, i.e., those that connect the forepart and the back, you allow ¼ inch more. The sleeve crown (or American 'cap') is cut ⅞ inch higher, so that it marries up with the extra length you've given the forepart and the back. The sleeves are also cut ⅝ inch wider through the forearm, which in tailoring terminology refers to the front of the sleeve. And then, of course, additional fabric is afforded the bottom of the coat to achieve the customer's desired length. A final cutting consideration is the overcoat's 'wrap', which is the extent to which its breast panels overlap each other. On a regular lounge coat, the wrap is normally 1¾ inches. On an overcoat, we tend to make it between 3 and 3½ inches, depending on the customer's size. Such overlap, after all, contributes to keeping the customer warm.

Sometimes, instead of something neutral like the covert coat, customers come in asking for an overcoat that will stand out. And so when we received, a few years ago, a catalogue sent by Holland & Sherry featuring an oversized

*Knee-length double-breasted oversized Prince of Wales check overcoat, styled by Barry Kamen.*

black-and-white Prince of Wales check, my mind immediately turned to an overcoat. Weighing in at the heavier end of the spectrum (25½ ounces/725 grams), the fabric was actually part of Holland & Sherry's dual-purpose range, useful for both suiting and home furnishing, suggesting it would have the hardiness outerwear requires. As ever with checked material, one must order a little extra and strike the fabric with a bit of an allowance for matching up the pattern at the seams. If the checks are relatively large, as in this case, we typically add 25 centimetres to each length; when they're smaller, 10 centimetres. Bearing in mind that black-and-white and red always make an eye-catching combination, we decided to make two coats out of the large-checked material: a single-breasted coat in light scarlet, and the double-breasted black-and-white model seen here. We gave the black-and-white coat straight-across pockets with a flap, buttons in a natural grey staghorn and a grey Bemberg lining. More recently, Maya Jauslin, one of our apprentices here at the shop, used the same black-and-white material to make a single-breasted overcoat with a shawl collar and a side-body back. These features are extremely unusual on an overcoat, but they looked beautiful, especially when paired with a bright red suit, and consequently Maya was named a finalist in the Merchant Taylors' biannual Golden Shears competition – the Oscars of the tailoring world. As for the scarlet single-breasted model we made up as well: less than a week after we put it in the window a young Chinese gentleman came in to buy it off the dummy and we haven't seen it since.

*Above: Maya Jauslin's single-breasted overcoat made from the same oversized black-and-white check material, and paired with a bright red suit to striking effect at the Golden Shears competition.*

*Top: The oversized high-contrast black-and-white check makes this otherwise classic overcoat anything but conservative. Inset: Original fashion sketch with 'button two no show' style.*

*Above: Other details include straight pockets with a 2¼-inch flap (top)
and three-button cuffs with plain black horn buttons (inset). Opposite:
The heavy black-and-white fabric from Holland & Sherry can be used
for upholstry as well as suiting.*

150

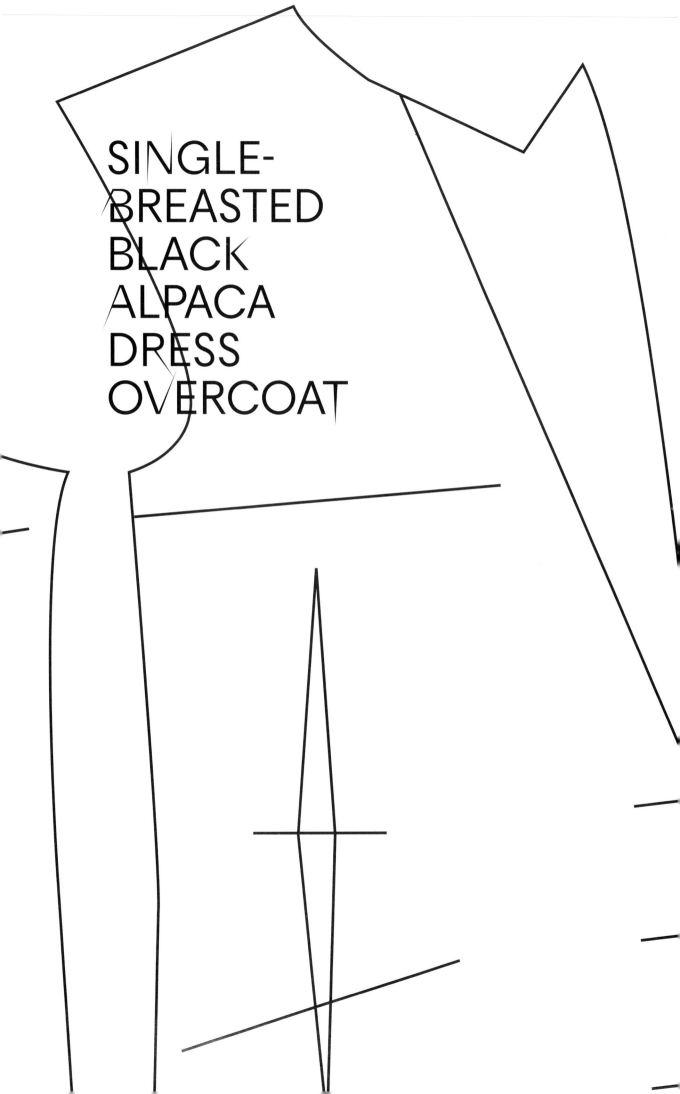

SINGLE-
BREASTED
BLACK
ALPACA
DRESS
OVERCOAT

There are few fabrics more luxurious than alpaca, also known as 'the Fibre of the Gods'. This natural fleece harvested from the alpaca, a domesticated species of the South American camelid, resembling a small llama, is a soft yet durable fibre similar to sheep's wool but warmer, shinier and more resilient, and hypoallergenic because it doesn't contain lanolin. Alpaca fabric is also naturally water-repellent and difficult to ignite. Since ancient times, alpaca have been kept in domesticated herds that graze throughout the year in the high-altitude Andes mountains of southern Peru, northern Bolivia, Ecuador and northern Chile. They are raised mainly for their fibre, as they are too small to be pack-animals, and are sheared once a year, during spring. The process by which yarn and cloth are produced from the resulting fleece is similar to that used for Merino wool. Alpaca comes in no fewer than 22 natural colours, which can also be dyed. The only drawback is that alpaca tends to be expensive, contributing to its reputation as an opulent material, prized for its silky handle and unusual, slightly shaggy look.

One of our favourite cloth suppliers, Scabal, founded in 1938 and conveniently located right next door to us here on Savile Row, produces a gorgeous range of alpaca in black, dark grey and tobacco. The material weighs about 20 ounces (565 grams) and is a blend of 72% alpaca and 28% wool. Its long, satiny pile bespeaks luxury and even flamboyance – think Old Hollywood. Seduced ourselves by the fabric's handle and lustre, we decided in the autumn of 2012 to do an alpaca promotion, centered on a formal two-piece dinner suit. But then we asked ourselves: what do you wear over a suit of such sumptuous material, without detracting from its glamour? And that's when we came up with the idea of a single-breasted dress overcoat in Scabal's alpaca. Liberace himself probably would have been among the first in line.

It's highly unusual, these days, to make an overcoat out of a relatively long-haired material; such an opulent garment would tend to be worn for only very formal occasions, so as to preserve it as long as possible. Still, since putting our first alpaca overcoat in the window in 2012, we've sold approximately a dozen of them, most in dark grey, which is the most versatile option – but also a few in black, like the somewhat more formal model you see here. In order to cut an overcoat you have to convert a customer's standard suitcoat pattern by increasing the front edge by 1 inch, dropping both back and forward shoulder by ⅞ inch on each side and letting out the side seams by ¼ inch, double all through. The sleeve will have to be adapted to the new scye (armhole) by adding ⅝ inch through the forearm, ⅝ – ⅞ inch to the crown and ⅞ inch to the

*A herd of alpaca, which produce one of the most luxurious coat materials available.*

153

top of the hindarm, reducing to nothing at the cuff. Moreover, when working with such a long pile (cashmere is similar), you have to cut the fabric all in the same way, to avoid shading (as with checks) and also the feeling of the fibre going the 'wrong way' under your hands when you smooth them down your clothes. We've also made a couple of double-breasted alpaca coats, but most have been single-breasted, which simplifies, or tones down, a material that is already quite formal. The coat is fly-fronted, which means its buttons are invisible, for an even more streamlined look. Typically I pair the coat with a black silk lining and occasionally I give it a velvet collar. Nine out of ten times we forego a breast pocket and equip the garment with just two straight-across hip pockets with a flap.

*Above: Fashion sketch showing fly-front (left) and button three (right) styles. Opposite: Our opulent, impeccably formal black alpaca overcoat.*

Today, in our less ceremonious times, the formal overcoat is something of an endangered species. Most men wear their usual everyday overcoat over a dress suit or even to black- or white-tie occasions, which, after all, are becoming less common. But back in my early years at Huntsman we still made lots of formal dress overcoats – as well as capes, which could also be worn over dresswear in milder weather. For example, we made a dress cape for Senator John Warner and also for his friend Sherman Unger to wear to Richard Nixon's inauguration. There was also a black barathea cape with a scarlet collar and lining for Cornel Lumière, as well as a scarlet one with a black collar and lining – i. e., the reverse – for his wife. Dame Margot Fonteyn famously wore a black barathea ladies' cape, a dramatic garment projecting an otherworldly aura. It simply wasn't proper back then among society's

upper echelons to wear anything so casual as everyday tweed to an evening ball. Cashmere was much more correct, if not the superluxurious vicuña. People simply had more opportunities to wear them, and they enjoyed upholding the exclusive standards that dictated elegance at any cost.

The alpaca dress overcoat has been popular primarily with my middle-aged customers – no one under 30 has ordered one, and no one over 65 – who like to conduct life with a bit of flair. The celebrated and charismatic American magician J. B. Benn, for example, has ordered one. He's performed for Henry Kissinger, Moby, Sia and Al Sharpton, to name a prestigious few, and it's always a pleasure to see and fit him at the Carlyle on one of our thrice-yearly trips to New York. If he has time at the end of our session together, he'll perform a trick for me, which is always a fabulous and surreal experience. As I've said, the price of an alpaca coat is not cheap, but Mr Benn's website boasts of his ability to 'change a dollar into a euro, a peso, a rupee, or any currency you name', which may explain things.

*Above: King George V and other dignitaries wearing classic dress overcoats at the Richmond Horse Show. Opposite: Details on our coat are kept simple, to showcase the opulence of the alpaca material.*

# REGALIA

# REDUX

SINGLE-
BREASTED
TWO-BUTTON
FROCK COAT
IN BLACK
BARATHEA

The frock coat was a standard form of dress during the Victorian and Edwardian eras and is distinguished by its 'skirt', which goes all the way around the wearer's legs just above (or at) the knee. (By contrast, the skirt on a morning coat, another common dress coat of the same period, is cut away in the front, leaving the man's trouser thighs visible; *see pages 166–71*.) A frock coat can be single- or double-breasted; the latter style is sometimes referred to as a Prince Albert coat, having come into fashion on both sides of the Atlantic after the eponymous prince appeared in one

on a visit to the United States. Frock coats were worn on much the same sort of occasions to which a man would wear a lounge suit today: weddings, funerals, baptisms, formal dinner parties and almost always to the office – indeed, in Victorian times the frock coat was standard business attire. More formal events called for a double-breasted frock coat with a peaked lapel, while the single-breasted model with a step- or notched lapel tended to be reserved for more informal outings. This was the sartorial law of the land until the more casual Newmarket coat, a type of morning coat typically worn for horse-riding, began to supplant the frock coat as acceptable daytime dress.

Cutting a frock coat – or, indeed, any body coat – is a rather more delicate and technical prospect than cutting a modern lounge coat. There are two main areas to be brought to attention. Firstly the coat is cut more closely to the body, the scye being approximately ¼–½ inch smaller than that of the equivalent lounge coat, in tandem with a trim chest and fitted side seam. The back is divided and cut into a side-body style, again to help with the suppression through the waist, but also to enable the coat to hug the back without showing any excess lengths. This contributes to a very smooth, wrinkle-free silhouette, with no fabric hanging or standing away from the body. Secondly, the balance of the body coat is very much dictated by the hang of the skirt, which should fall straight from the waist seam as opposed to running off or running on. It's in part for this reason that a relatively heavy material tends to be used when making up a frock coat: something in the range of 14–15 ounces (400–425 grams) tends to work best.

*An elegant Victorian gentleman in a double-breasted 'Prince Albert' frock coat, c. 1903.*

When I was engaged to be married, I decided to make myself a frock coat to wear to my wedding. Or rather, I asked my Huntsman mentor Brian Hall to help me make one, recreating as closely as possible the frock coat he'd made for Dennis Price to wear in the film *Kind Hearts and Coronets* (1949). This was a single-breasted, two-button black barathea model, as you see here, and which I wore with a cream waistcoat and black wool dogtooth check trousers with a very slim fit. Not wanting to take up any other colleagues' time with my personal business (on Savile Row there remains even today a bit of stigma attached to private work), I employed a tailor from Gieves & Hawkes to make up the coat for me, but he put the biggest rope I'd ever seen on the sleeves, such that they puffed up at the shoulders almost as much as the ones that Princess Diana wore to her wedding. In a panic, for I was due to get married in only a few days, I asked Colin Hammick for help, and he valiantly entrusted the problem to Reno Inglima, one of Huntsman's very best tailors. Inglima righted the job with time to spare, and on the big day I felt triumphant in my bespoke throwback to a nobler time – but so much for keeping my personal life out of my work.

My marital frock coat had what we call an inset facing on the lapel, which means the lapel itself was made of the same black barathea as the rest of the suit but had a visible inset made of black corded silk rather heavier than the plain silk used for the coat's lining. ('Corded' means that the silk had a slightly ribbed effect, commonly referred to in America as 'grosgrain'.) The coat also had four-button 'formed cuffs,' which are narrower than regular cuffs and seamed 4 or 5 inches up from the bottom – a typical style feature of the frock coat. Indeed, with a formal style like this, one tends not to stray too far from the traditional ingredients, though in the spirit of modernity I would certainly be keen to experiment with any alternative embellishments, or with any fabric of sufficient weight. I haven't made a frock coat since my own, unfortunately, but I do hold out hope that one day soon it might roar back into fashion. Meanwhile, my wife has taken to wearing the one I made for our wedding as an overcoat, a look I must admit she pulls off beautifully.

*Details of the author's black barathea frock coat, including corded silk facing (top left and right) and 4-inch formed cuff with four hand-worked holes and corded silk buttons (bottom left and right).*

*Fashion sketch and mannequin shot showing two-button front, waist seam and peaked lapel with inset facings.*

*Back details of the coat: side-body back, waist seam and skirt.*

TARTAN
MORNING
COAT

I n the early twentieth century, the frock coat gave way to the morning coat as the most common form of men's dress. Today it is worn only at very formal events, such as weddings, or to the best seats at Ascot, but once upon a time its slightly rounded, cutaway front – a development that afforded horseback riders more freedom of leg movement – made it a relatively 'casual' alternative to its predecessor. Like frock coats, morning coats are cut with a side-body back, which means that the back is divided into two rounded panels that give the garment added shape into the small of the back and through the waist at the side seam. The length of the tails is dictated by the back of the customer's knee, plus 1 inch. Technically, this produces the 'correct' length, though I have been asked by one or two customers to extend it slightly – a deviation from classic proportions that may seem minor but that my more conservative colleagues at Huntsman probably would have resisted.

These days, the most commonly chosen fabrics for a three-piece suit in traditional 'morning grey' are grey worsted or pick-and-pick, also known as sharkskin: a smooth twill weave worsted with a very fine two-toned appearance slightly more elegant than a normal worsted. The most formal version of the morning coat, however, remains the black model, typically combined with a grey, cream or pale blue waistcoat and striped trousers. Contrary to the frock coat, which may be either single- or double-breasted, a morning coat is always single-breasted. But just as with the frock coat (and, indeed, any body coat), balance considerations dictate that you avoid using a material that's too light: we recommend a minimum of 14 ounces (400 grams). If a customer wants black, we suggest a black barathea or a tight black herringbone. If he wants grey, we propose a grey worsted that's clean-cut, which is to say that its 'hair' has been shaved close to the surface. In the normal run of things, one doesn't stray too far from these two time-honoured ideals.

Moreover, when deviations are made to the hallowed morning coat they tend to be understated. One example is the black morning coat that Prince Charles wore in 2005 for his wedding to Camilla Parker Bowles. The ensemble was conventional enough: black coat, light grey double-breasted waistcoat with a cream vest slip, grey patterned tie, a light blue striped shirt with a white collar, and charcoal-grey striped trousers probably held up by fishtail braces. (These feature on 95% of morning-suit trousers.) But the Prince of Wales's coat, which had been made by one of my esteemed

*Prince Charles, wearing a black morning coat with unusual black braiding along its front edge, at his wedding to Camilla Parker Bowles in 2005.*

167

Savile Row colleagues, Anderson & Sheppard's chief cutter Mr Hitchcock, also had an unusual feature: black braiding along its front edge. This is actually a detail that was popular many decades ago but is rare in modern times – or at least it was rare until the Prince exhibited it at Windsor Guildhall. Suddenly, we received a flurry of orders for black morning coats edged with black braiding, and some of my customers even brought in coats I'd made for them years earlier to have the braiding added. It was as though permission had been granted to revolutionize, however subtly, a beloved classic.

At Richard Anderson – where on average we make about twenty morning coats a year – I have decided to take that permission one step further to create a truly original morning coat: in tartan. This light fawn-based, all-wool 12–13 ounce (340–370 gram) tartan was given to me many years ago by an old tailor friend who worked at Kilgour. One reason tartan and the morning coat seem a natural pairing is that tartan is typically associated with the Scottish kilt. And although it originated in the sixteenth century as the traditional dress of men and boys in the Scottish Highlands (and today is experiencing something of a renaissance in popular urban fashion), the kilt has for many decades been largely reserved for formal occasions, such as weddings – which are also, of course, where you'd be most likely to see a morning coat. Furthermore, the crisscross pattern that characterizes tartan

*Engravings of different styles of fashionable morning coats from* Victorian trade journal The Tailor and Cutter, *1874–75.*

*Our fawn tartan morning coat with cream Ermazine lining.*
*The crisscross pattern accentuates the contoured cut.*

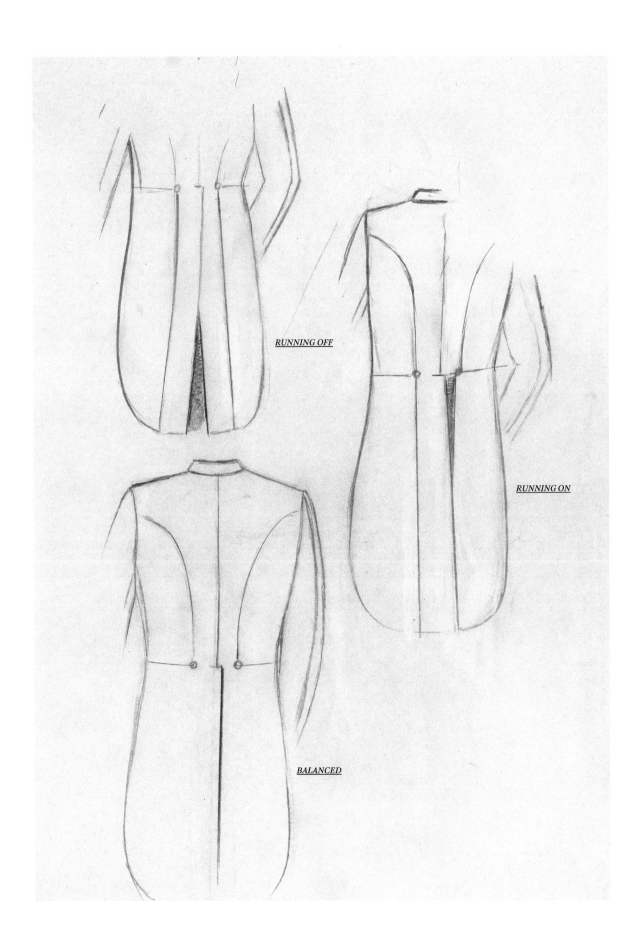

RUNNING OFF

RUNNING ON

BALANCED

lends itself well to the morning coat pattern, in that its geometry accentuates the curved cut of the side bodies, whereas when they are cut from a solid-coloured fabric, side bodies are less noticeable and therefore more difficult to appreciate. One must pay special attention to matching up the checks as closely as possible at the seams, but as this is a concern whenever working with check or plaid, it's certainly not an inordinate obstacle here.

As in a black or grey morning coat, to which we add a lining that matches the exterior but is quilted on the inside chest for a sense of luxury and a slightly stiffer shape, we have given our tartan morning coat a cream Ermazine lining that matches the colour of the tartan's background. The lining also matches the clean-cut, cream-coloured worsted wool trousers with which we recommend pairing the coat. And, to finish everything off: a glove pocket in the skirt. This is something we add to approximately 20% of the morning coats we make, to accommodate the wearer's handwear when he takes it off to make notes on his racecard – or, perhaps, to kiss the bride's hand when she exits the church.

*Above: Detail of outbreast pocket and tartan material. Inset: Sketch illustrating correct and incorrect hanging skirts.*

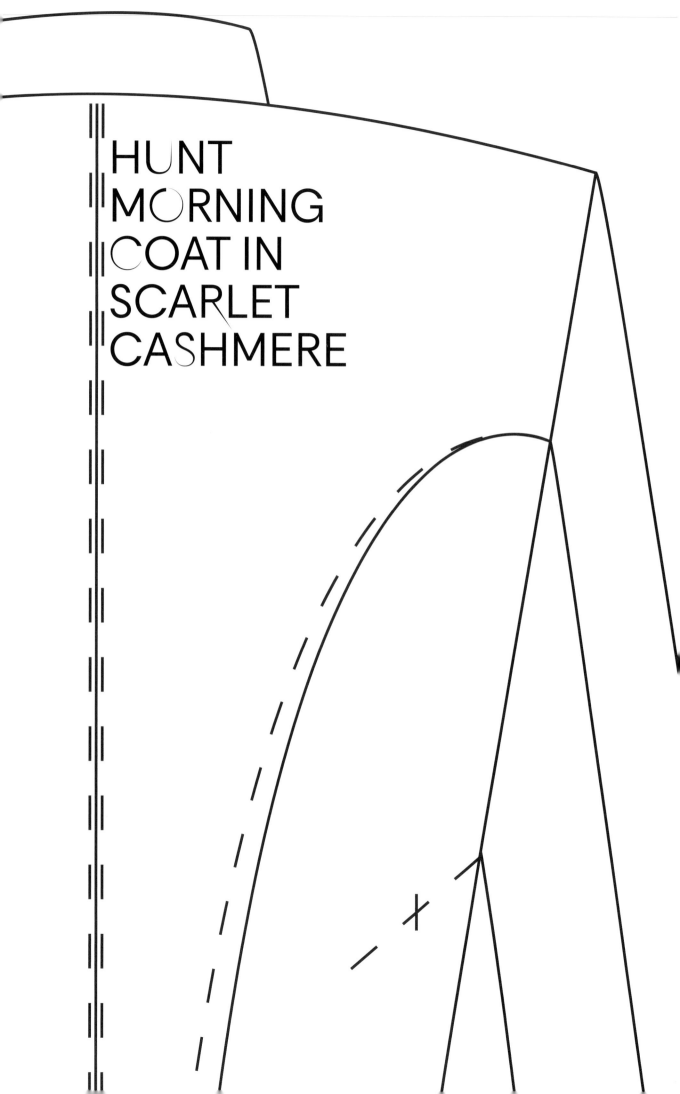

HUNT
MORNING
COAT IN
SCARLET
CASHMERE

Another form of body coat – a coat that hugs the figure with the help of side bodies, and that has a waist seam and a skirt – is the classic hunt coat. The pursuit of a fox by trained hounds and unarmed followers on horseback, fox-hunting originated in the sixteenth century and was practised legally in England and Wales until it was banned by a highly controversial law effective from February 2005. Prior to the ban, the Savile Row houses that made hunt coats could expect to receive orders for as many as 50 hunt coats a year; now, although certain modified forms of the sport remain legal under British law ('for the purpose of enabling a bird of prey to hunt the wild mammal', for example), and fox-hunting is still permitted in other countries including Australia, Canada, France, Ireland, Italy and the United States, the demand for bespoke hunt coats has fallen significantly. We've made only a handful of true hunt coats here at No. 13 in the last ten years. Dege & Skinner, one of the oldest institutions on Savile Row – the house has been family-owned since its incipience in 1865 and its managing director, William Skinner, is chairman of the Savile Row Bespoke Association – has long been recognized for its superb hunt coats and probably makes more of them than anyone else today. One reason is that in addition to its British clients it also has a strong relationship with customers on the American Eastern Seaboard, where enthusiasm for the hunting tradition is alive and well, particularly in Middleburg, Virginia. Still, the number of orders Dege & Skinner receives today is significantly fewer than it would have filled during fox-hunting's heydey.

Then and now, inasmuch as hunting is still practised, there are specific rules governing who can wear what on a hunt. The classic red or scarlet colour, also known as 'hunter's pink' (some say because pink is the colour a scarlet coat takes on after years of weather and wear), is reserved for hunt staff, Masters of the sport and riders who have been given their hunting society's 'hunt button', a badge of recognition for helpfulness in the field. Before he is awarded a hunt button, a man may wear a plain black coat with plain black Vulcanite buttons. After receiving his hunt button, he is entitled to wear a red coat and brass buttons, with the number of buttons on the front of the coat further indicating his status: three buttons for hunt subscribers, four for Masters, and five for Huntsmen and Whippers-in (hunt staff). Hunt-specific coats can also have a contrasting collar, and some are in colours other than the traditional red: green, mustard, or, as in the case of the famous Duke of Beaufort hunt, navy with a buff collar. Typically, the three-button coats are

*Sketch of hunt coat showing front, back and collar details.*

*The scarlet cashmere hunt-style morning coat with three-button front,*
*outside ticket pocket, waist seam and rounded morning coat skirt.*

morning hunt coats and the four-button ones frock hunt coats, with five-button coats being much rarer, all but restricted to the Master who calls and owns the hunt. (I've also heard that five-button hunt coats are the exclusive domain of exceptionally tall people, though one wonders whether this isn't because Masters tend to be tall.) Prior to and following the season's main hunt, riders wear what's called 'ratcatcher' attire: an informal tweed coat-and-breeches ensemble whose name derives from Victorian times, when the crofter of a hunt and the local ratcatcher were both distinguishable by the terriers they used to track down foxes and rats, respectively; thus, the crofter or 'terrier man' also became known as a 'ratcatcher'.

A decade or so ago now, just a couple of years after the hunting ban had taken effect, an American expat now living England came in to see us with a length of scarlet cashmere given to him by a friend. He wanted us to use this cashmere to make up something eye-catching, and when in the course of admiring the material someone pointed out that it was identical in colour to traditional hunting pinks, the garment was decided. This customer had, in fact, been a keen hunter himself, and even had buttons he'd earned as a participant in the Vale of the White Horse hunt, so we decided to throw these in as well. As one might imagine, cashmere is a thoroughly impractical material with which to make up a coat for charging through the wind and rain, so in this case the point was merely to borrow the morning hunt coat style in order to create a kind of homage to the traditional design that would be worn mostly indoors. I loved the idea, which spoke directly to our theme of marrying tradition and modernity, and so I got to work at once.

As mentioned, when fitting a hunt coat, as with any coat destined to be worn while riding a horse (or a motorbike; *see page 117*), at Huntsman we would actually ask the customer to sit in an old saddle that we kept in the shop for that purpose, but at Richard Anderson we instead use a high-backed chair

*Traditional coats in hunting pink, these with contrasting green collars, worn as the Duke of Buccleuch's hounds are led by the hunt Master in a fox hunt in St Boswells, Scotland.*

turned round (Dege & Skinner uses a large globetrotter suitcase). The customer straddles the chair and leans forward slightly, as if pulling on the reins of a horse. It's this posture that dictates how in cutting the coat you must make the back a little wider, adding in the case of lighter materials ¼ inch on either side, and with heavier, less supple fabrics ⅜ inch. You also have to pitch the sleeves forward slightly and afford the back of each a bit of extra material. There is always only one vent in a hunt coat, with two buttons on the back and the positioning of the front buttons determined by where the coat's skirt separates

when the wearer is sitting in his riding position. On a morning hunt coat such as the one pictured here, the length of the skirt is dictated by where the customer's thumbnail falls when he's standing in a neutral position; the skirt must also splay and flow naturally over his legs when he's sitting in the saddle. Most hunt coats are made of a heavy, hard-wearing material such as melton or cavalry twill weighing in the range of 30–32 ounces (850–910 grams). Initially I was nervous as to whether our customer's scarlet cashmere would be heavy enough to achieve the right balance, but weighing in at just over the minimum 14 ounces (400 grams) that we typically recommend for body coats, it performed beautifully.

In addition to giving it the customer's own hunt buttons, we finished off this model with a red cashmere collar. We also gave its upper half a lightweight lining in plain red silk and a ventile cotton lining in the skirt. This is contrary to 'normal' hunt coats, which for warmth tend to feature a heavy gingham-check shirting in the torso, heavy melton in the skirt, and, to cut down on friction, Bemburg lining in sleeves. The cuffs on our cashmere model have two buttons each, and there is a small ticket pocket on the outside of the skirt. There are also two inbreast pockets and – hidden inside the skirt – two large poacher's pockets, each held up by a tab and button (*see page 113*). You won't see this coat atop a thoroughbred in the Vale of the White Horse anytime soon, but for those mourning the hunting ban it does seem to evoke a sort of British serenity with respect to the circumstances. In other words: keep calm and carry on.

*Above: An illustration from* Vanity Fair *showing Mr Edgar Lubbock, Master of the Blankney Hunt, in a four-button hunt coat, c. 1906.*

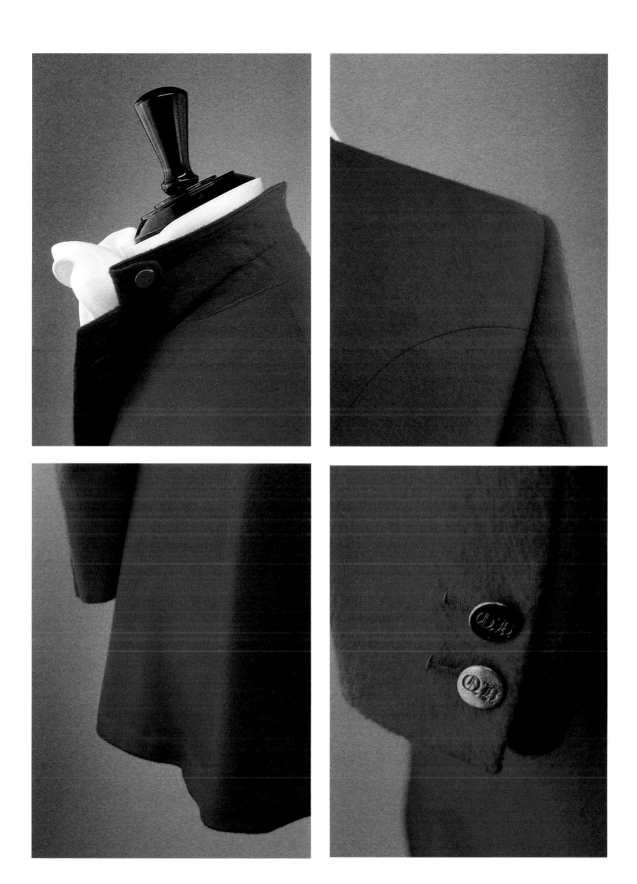

*Above: Details of our coat, including tab-and-button collar underturn (top left), side-body back seam 'marrying up' to hindarm seam (top right), fall and drape at skirt (bottom left), and two-button cuff with Vale of the White Horse hunt buttons (bottom right).*

CHARCOAL
NEHRU
COAT WITH
POLKA-DOT
LINING

The Nehru coat derives from the Indian *achkan* or *sherwani* garments frequently worn by Jawaharlal Nehru, prime minister of India from 1947 until 1964. Western iterations tend to be much shorter than the traditional knee-length *achkan* that can have as many as eight buttons running from neck to waist, but essentially they feature the same distinctive mandarin collar: a short stand-up collar that evokes those associated with mandarins in Imperial China. The same type of collar is frequently seen on chefs' coats, perhaps because it protects the wearer's neck from burns and stains, and also makes the coat reversible.

(This is the same reason that many chefs' uniforms are double-breasted.) Stand or mandarin-type collars also commonly feature on certain modern military uniforms, including those of the US Army, because they make the jacket easier to wear under crew vests and body armour; furthermore, the extra coverage helps to prevent neck chafing by these outer garments. Versions of the mandarin collar are also seen on Catholic clerical uniforms, such as cassocks, in some cases in the same asymmetrical button-band style as on the American army jackets. In other clerical cases the collar is 'notched' in the middle and closed with a loop or a hook.

Despite the mandarin collar's ecclesiastical connotations, the makers of James Bond films seemed to think it had a sinister, futuristic look, and incorporated it in the costumes of many of 007's nemeses, from Dr No to Ernst Stavro Blofeld and Kamal Khan, as well as those of Bond himself. The Beatles famously wore matching khaki Nehru-style jackets in front of more than 55,000 concert-goers at Shea Stadium in 1965. Such pop-culture appropriations of the Nehru coat sealed its appeal, and by the time I arrived at Huntsman in the early 1980s the house was in the habit of making as many as six Nehru coats a year, including two sets for the famous Modern Jazz Quartet: one in grey silk for a European tour; the other in white wool with black braiding down the matching trousers.

For the most part, cutting a Nehru coat is very similar to cutting a standard lounge coat; the trickier aspects are entirely in reconfiguring the neck and chest. First, one must give a new run to the back, by lowering the back neck a good ¼ inch at the centre and simultaneously raising it by a good ¼ inch at the side, running into nothing at the shoulder end. Second, the front shoulder at the forepart must be straightened by approximately

*Joseph Wiseman wearing a Nehru-style coat as Dr No in the eponymous*
*Bond film (1962).*

¾ inch, and the chest reduced to compensate. The collar's height tends to be between 1 and 1¼ inch, depending on the size of the customer's neck. Typically the cuffs have three or four buttons, though we've also made Nehru coats with only one button on each cuff and others with buttonless turned-up cuffs, which make for a more unusual, formal look. Unless the customer wishes to emulate the original longer *achkan* design, the length of the coat tends to be the same as that of a lounge coat, and it can have one, two or no vents in the back – two, as ever, affording the most ease and comfort when the wearer sits down.

The Nehru coat featured here is made of our own in-house charcoal-coloured worsted in a medium weight: 13 ounces (370 grams). We've given it two inside pockets plus two invisible vertical pockets at the side seams and one welted outbreast pocket, this last being the only pocket visible on the outside. The coat has two vents in the back, four buttons concealed by a fly front, and a hook-and-eye closure at the neck. All of these minimalist features contribute to a very clean, streamlined look that allows us to be a little more daring with the lining, in this case a striking white-on-magenta polka-dot Ermazine.

Today, the Nehru coat is especially popular at Indian weddings, where many men wear silk or slubbed-silk models (paired with matching trousers) that often feature silk knots in lieu of buttons. But the style is also prominent at non-Indian weddings as well, and for that matter at all manner of formal and informal occasions, as the Nehru coat is equally easy to combine with casual clothing. It can be worn with jeans, over a button-down shirt with an open collar or over a t-shirt with the collar's hook-and-eye closed. One reason for the Nehru coat's growing popularity may be that its collar renders unnecessary the addition of a necktie. It's also a singularly unfussy garment that, much like a smoking jacket, can be made in practically any fabric the customer fancies, from the classic silk models

*Detail of charcoal worsted fabric, stand collar and buttons concealed by the fly-front closure*

*Above: Magenta polka-dot Ermazine lining (top) and internal fly-front (inset).*

already mentioned to the worsted wool seen here, or mohair, fresco, crepe, gabardine, cashmere, tweed or corduroy. When he met with President Obama in 2015, Nehru's descendant Prime Minister Narendra Modi went so far as to wear a bespoke six-button Nehru coat and matching trousers made of a unique navy pinstripe commissioned from Holland & Sherry. From a distance, the stripes looked like true pinstripes of solid gold, but close-up one sees that in fact they comprise the prime minister's name: NARENDRA DAMODARDAS MODI, embroidered vertically over and over. The suit later entered the Guinness World Records as the most expensive suit ever sold at an auction – for 43,131,311 rupees, or almost £450,000.

*Above: Mannequin shot of our Nehru coat (top) and Sean Connery wearing a similar coat, but with visible buttons, as James Bond in* Dr No *(1962) (inset).*

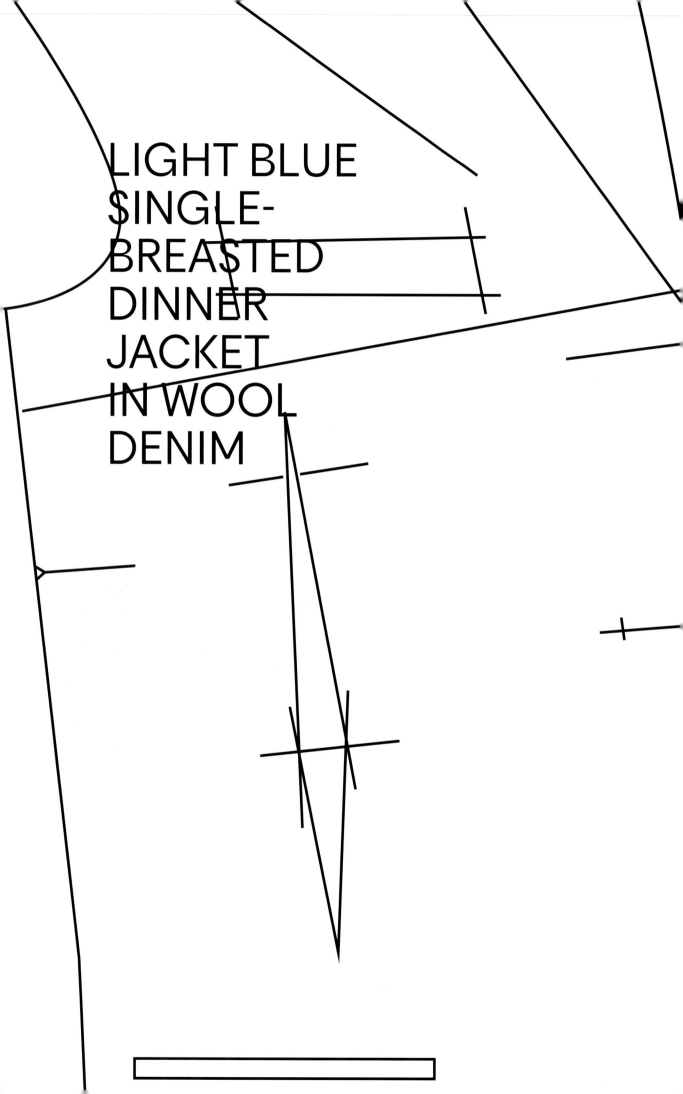

LIGHT BLUE
SINGLE-
BREASTED
DINNER
JACKET
IN WOOL
DENIM

W hen I worked at Huntsman in the 1980s and '90s, it was rare for one of our distinguished customers not to own a dinner jacket. This quintessentially formal garment is said to have been invented just two doors down, at No. 15 Savile Row, by Henry Poole, in 1865, when the Prince of Wales and future King Edward VII asked his tailor and friend to cut 'a short celestial blue evening coat to be worn at informal dinners at Sandringham'. Known in American parlance as a tuxedo, or 'tux' – a term that originated in the States around 1888, when variations on the prince's model came to be seen in Tuxedo Park, a Hudson Valley hotspot for New York's social elite – such black-tie finery was *de*

*rigueur* for any serious Savile Row clotheshorse. Between us, my Huntsman forerunners and I made black-tie dinner suits for Gianni Agnelli, the Duke of Beaufort, Gregory Peck, Dirk Bogarde, Omar Sharif, Peter Sellers and Rex Harrison, among countless others. With rare exceptions, these dinner suits were all either plain black or midnight blue – in Dormeuil mohair, say, and with a grosgrain silk or satin facing that matched the buttons' fabric and the trousers' braiding. Typically, it was easier to find a bowtie and cummerbund to match facing that was black, but both black and blue facing were common and looked equally divine. James Bond fans will note that 007 has displayed a reliable penchant for midnight-blue dinner suits over the years, as modelled by Sean Connery, George Lazenby, Roger Moore, Daniel Craig and Pierce Brosnan (whose suit in *Tomorrow Never Dies* has blue facing, whereas the ones he wore in *The World is Not Enough* and *Die Another Day* are faced in black). Whatever their colour, dinner jackets are traditionally worn with matching black or blue trousers, completing a look that has changed very little in the last century and indeed remains the gold standard of sartorial elegance.

Still, since opening Richard Anderson Ltd in 2001, I've made traditional dinner suits less frequently than I did at Huntsman. I suspect this is a trend reflecting, more than anything, our less formal times. One of the first dinner jackets we made here at No. 13 was a midnight-blue model for Sir Ian McKellen, who came to us for something to wear to the Academy Awards when he was nominated for his role as Gandalf in *Lord of the Rings*. (Ironically, we are indebted to Versace for the commission, for Versace had sent Sir Ian some flowers congratulating him on his nod and suggesting he wear Versace to the ceremony, but the actor wasn't at home, so a neighbour

*Fashion sketch for blue denim dinner jacket showing contrasting black facings on the lapel.*

collected the bouquet and brought it round later with the suggestion that Sir Ian instead have something made by *his* tailor – me.) We also made a suit for Tate Taylor to wear to the Oscars, sans bowtie, when he was nominated in 2012 for directing *The Help*. But increasingly, unless you're an award nominee or a conductor at the Royal Opera House, you'll notice that you have fewer opportunities to don a tuxedo these days, as *cravate noire* weekday dinners and even formal weddings have become things of the past. It bears mentioning that black tie is not even the most formal men's dress code in the modern Western world – that title goes to *white* tie, a.k.a. *full* evening dress, a style dating back to the end of the eighteenth century and favoured by Beau Brummell, the father of English dandyism, a man who allegedly took five hours a day to dress and recommended polishing one's boots with champagne.

*Above: Mannequin shot of our denim dinner jacket. Opposite: Pierce Brosnan wearing a classic black dinner jacket in the James Bond film* Tomorrow Never Dies *(1997) (top); and Ian McKellen wearing one of ours to the 2002 Academy Awards (inset).*

Naturally, then, my mind has turned toward ways of experimenting with the form for more modern purposes. If you're going to invest in a dinner jacket, you want it to be made of an elegant-looking material, but also one that is durable enough to last. As mentioned, mohair is a common choice, as well as wool barathea, although the interaction of mohair with light tends to give barathea a more luminescent look. In the autumn of 2002, however, in anticipation of the holiday party season, we began making dinner jackets in slightly less formal fabrics. One was a 10-ounce (285-gram) cotton-cashmere blend in charcoal grey, another a light blue 11–12 ounce (310–340 gram) wool-and-denim mixture made by Zegna and pictured here. The denim mix has a slightly narrower wale than the cash-cot blend, which is to say its corrugated surface – the grooved texture associated with corduroy and denim – contains fewer ridges per inch. In both cases, we gave the jacket a peaked lapel in black satin facing as well as a single black satin button on the front and four on each cuff. The trousers, made of black mohair, feature a single satin braid down each leg.

The result is a supremely elegant ensemble but also one that could be deconstructed to achieve a more casual look – for example, by wearing the jacket with a plain white shirt, jeans, boots or even trainers. That said, one must be careful pairing denim with denim: the blues should either match very closely or be sufficiently different from each another so as not to clash. Alternatively, for a more dandified effect, you can combine the jacket with a ruffled shirt, oversized bowtie and pocket square. I made a jacket similar to this for Rocky Mazzilli, the son of Tiziano and Louise Mazzilli, owners of Voyage, the infamous erstwhile Fulham Road clothing boutique. Indeed, the significantly lighter blue of this model – relative to 007's nearly black midnight hue – is a look that both pays tribute to the Prince of Wales's original 'celestial' model and also seems to have a special appeal to our younger customers of today. Certainly it's a style for those who aren't afraid to turn heads when they stride into a champagne reception. To which I say: Cheers!

*Details include a 3⅜-inch peaked lapel with black corded-silk facings and lapel hole made by hand (top), and a natural roll into the one-button closure (inset).*

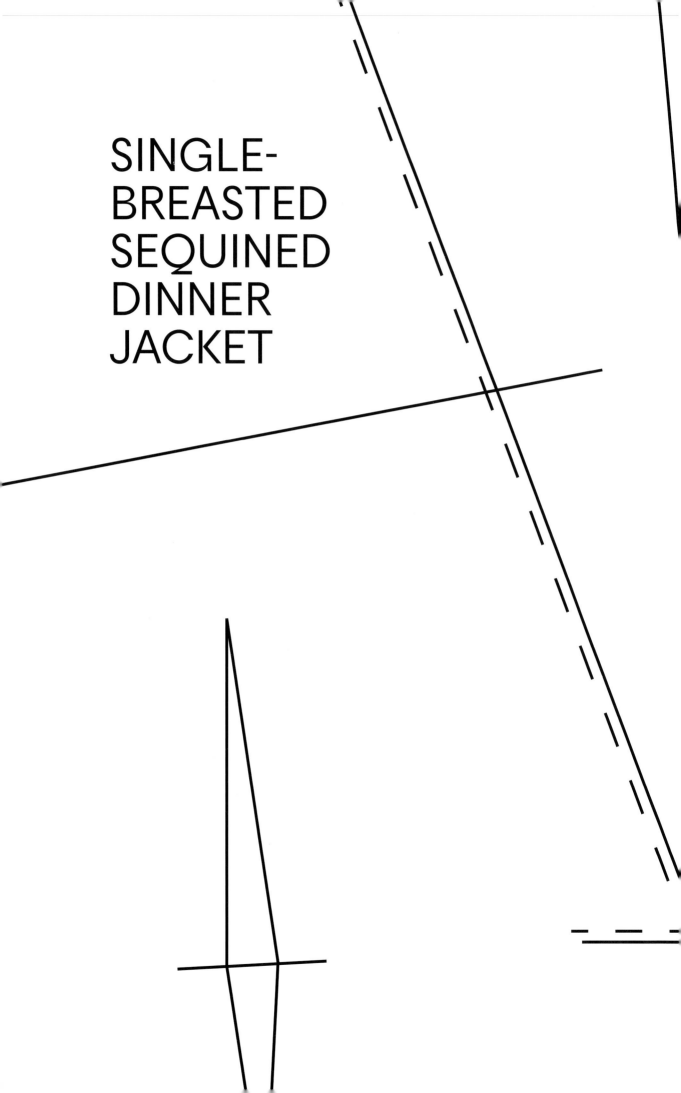

SINGLE-
BREASTED
SEQUINED
DINNER
JACKET

I t was in late 2005 that I went into Soho's Broadwick Silks looking for a bit of inspiration for our Christmas window display. I wanted to create an iconic coat, one that would combine the clean, classic silhouette I'd learned at Hunstman with an undeniably modern ingredient. Rummaging around among the usual checks and worsteds I came across a piece of black sequined fabric that I could not resist purchasing and bringing back to the shop; I wanted to see what Carmelo Reina, my 76-year-old Italian coatmaker, could do with it, in terms of making it up. Reina is not your average coatmaker, most of whom would balk at working with material that is even the slightest bit difficult. At 66, after working 25 years on Savile Row at our old alma mater Hunstman, he retired, but after only six months in his native Sicily called to

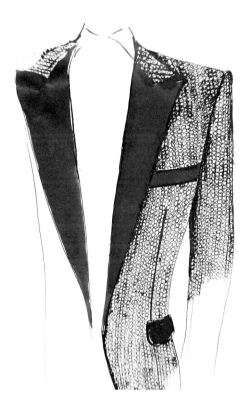

ask whether I could use an extra coatmaker; he was bored with the leisure life and wanted to come back. I was glad to take him on, and not least because he does it for the love of the job. Reina thrives on challenges, and within a fortnight he'd transformed my pattern and 2 metres 10 of black sequins from Broadwick into our first ever glittering dinner jacket. An icon was born.

The cut of this coat differs from our classic line in three basic ways: 1) it's a bit shorter, as befits the jazzy material and also because shorter lengths are common during economic recessions, I think because they suggest restraint; 2) it has a peaked, or rather double-breasted lapel, rather than a single-breasted one, to give it an air of formality; and 3) it has flaps on the pockets, whereas most tailoring houses would never add pocket flaps to a dinner jacket, but which I thought beneficial here because the little bit of extra silk helps to balance out all that glitz. We did have to make two concessions, given the nature of the material: the shoulders and sleeves, normally put in by hand, had to be machine-sewn on for a cleaner seam, and instead of a true buttonhole on the front and cuffs, we had to sew on purely decorative buttons and add a simple hook-and-eye catch to hold the coat together.

When the model was done, we put it up in the shop window and sat back to wait.

Immediately, it began to attract attention. People were shy at first; they loved the look but seemed a bit nervous about actually donning it themselves. Then Sebastian Horsley came in, and, after trying on the window model, decided it was just the thing for his *Dandy in the Underworld* book tour. Horsley needed no excuse to wear sequins; he was a fixture on the streets of Soho in cerulean velour, painted fingernails and a top hat – and in fact

*Fashion sketch for the sequined dinner jacket showing contrasting facings, outbreast welt and pocket flaps.*

he ordered not one but two sequined coats: one black and one red. Both had a slightly altered cut, as he wanted a more 'casual' jacket style, as opposed to the dinner jacket model: no facing on the lapels and no pocket flaps – just sequins, and plenty of them. He wanted matching trousers as well, which because of the material's fragility we designed to be as simple as possible: no pockets, a zip fly and an elastic waistband.

Shortly thereafter Bryan Ferry walked into our shop for the first time and asked to try on the original window model, too. It was a touch small for him,

but he liked that: it looked 'cooler' that way and Ferry doesn't button his jackets onstage anyway, so the fact that it strained to close around him wasn't an issue. He bought it then and there, and began to wear it in concerts; *The Times* described him as 'resplendent in a black jacket that gleamed like the skin of an otter'. Four months later he ordered a second one, exactly the same, lest the first one wear out. We had Reina make up another model, and not long after that my business partner, Brian, was conducting our semi-annual meetings with customers at the Ritz-Carlton in Chicago and took an appointment with an 89-year-old doctor and war veteran named Fred Weil. Dr Weil arrived while Brian was finishing up with another one of our longtime clients, a highly successful public relations agent named Maribeth Kuzmeski, who, because her company is called Red Zone Marketing, orders her suits almost exclusively in red. Dr Weil mentioned that his family was going to throw him a ninetieth birthday party and he wanted something special to wear – a white tuxedo, or perhaps a dinner jacket in midnight blue. Then he saw the black sequined coat hanging up along with the others Brian had out on display. 'Oh go on,' said Brian. Dr Weil tried it on, and true to form Maribeth sealed the deal: 'Oh, you *have* to get it.' He did, and after the party sent us a photo, taken by the local paper, of himself wearing it.

I will admit that, in the beginning, I was a little apprehensive about the sequined coat, for while I wanted to create something fresh and fancy one must always be careful not to alienate one's existing clientele with styles that might seem more at home in Sin City than on Savile Row. But the reaction was overwhelmingly positive. In addition to the above orders, we sold another twenty sequined coats and suits to old and new customers

*Above: The sequined dinner jacket is shorter than the classic model, and has a one-button dummy front with hook-and-loop closure due to the fragile material.*
*Opposite: Non-standard silk pocket flaps, added to balance out the glitzy material.*

*Bryan Ferry wearing his black sequined jacket, unbuttoned, at a concert at Wembley Stadium, 2007.*

alike; we also featured a silver model in the Savile Row Bespoke Exhibition at the British ambassador's residence in Paris, where it was a star of the show and went on to be worn by singer Rhydian (under a white fur coat) on the television programme *The X Factor*. Dismayingly, the fabric has been discontinued and its manufacturer now makes only a pale imitation of what I bought on Broadwick Street all those years ago: the sequins, stitching and backing are not as strong, making for a considerably less robust and flexible material. Which means that, until another company can be persuaded to take up the cause, the Richard Anderson otter skins already in circulation are a limited edition.

*Sebastian Horsley in 2007, wearing the red sequined jacket and matching trousers we made for him.*

# GLOSSARY

## A

*advance fitting* – See *forward fitting*.

*aerophane* – A fabric that resembles a fine silk gauze and was commonly used in the nineteenth century for pleated or gathered garments; it has also been used as a decorative element: for example, when embroidered or added as an appliqué.

*alpaca* – The soft, silky fleece (or fabric or yarn made from the fleece) of a South American camelid (hoofed mammal) related to the llama. Its colour is typically grey, russet or brown. Alpaca was first introduced to England by Benjamin Outram who spun a rough yarn with it and wove it into rugs and shawls.

*angling kit* – Fishing clothes.

## B

*back stitch* – A hand stitch in which the needle is 'backed up' and inserted at the end of the previous stitch.

*back strap* – A strap across the back of a garment, such as on a waistcoat.

*back tacking* – Reverse stitches at the beginning and end of a seam to give it strength.

*baize* – A woven wool or wool-nylon blend typically used for the surfacing of billiard tables. See also pages 123–24.

*balance* – Usually used in reference to the relationship between the front and back of a garment: the ideal harmony among two or more sections of a garment and its wearer's figuration.

*balance marks* – Notches, nips or threads in garment parts and which help to preserve the balance of the garment during assembly.

*bar tack* – Side-by-side stitches used at the ends of buttonholes, pocket corners and belt loops for reinforcement.

*barathea* – A soft fabric of silk, rayon, cotton or wool in a hopsack twilled weave, with a pebbled or ribbed surface. Worsted barathea is often used to make fine dress evening coats in black or midnight blue, whereas silk barathea is often used to make neckties.

*baste* – To sew a garment together temporarily with long, loose, provisional stitches, usually in white thread (for easy spotting during removal), early in the construction and fittings process.

*batiste* – A fine, often sheer fabric, constructed in either a plain or figured weave and made of various natural or synthetic materials. Named after Baptiste of Cambrai, who was supposedly its first maker.

*bearer* – Atop the fly, a piece of cloth stitched into the waistband of trousers for reinforcement and to bear the weight of the trousers when fastened.

*Bedford cord* – A smooth corded fabric with cords running lengthwise, probably originating in the town of Bedford, England.

*bellows pockets* – Pockets that expand thanks to their expansion pleats. See also pages 63, 67.

*Bemberg* – The brand name for a silky, semi-synthetic material, also called Cupro, which is durable and breathes well, making it an excellent lining. See also *Cupro*.

*bias* – A line running diagonal to the warp and weft threads of a cloth. True bias is at 45 degrees and is the angle of reference in cutting an undercollar.

*bicycled* – Slang adjective for work done on a sewing machine.

*birdseye* – Woven fabric having an all-over pattern of tiny geometric shapes reminiscent of a bird's eye. A pattern comprising larger 'eyes' is sometimes referred to as 'pheasant-eye'.

*blazer* – A single- or double-breasted sport coat, often adorned with metal (e.g., gilt or silver) buttons and sometimes an insignia indicating affiliation with a company or club.

*blend* – A yarn obtained when two or more staple fibres are combined in a textile process for producing spun yarns; or a fabric containing a blended yarn of the same fibre content in the warp and weft.

*blind fly* – A fly fastened down rather than left open between each button.

*blind stitch* – A stitch by hand or machine that does not penetrate all the way through the cloth.

*block pattern* – A generalized paper template for marking out the parts of a garment on cloth.

*bluff edges* – Finished edges in which no stitches are visible on the garment's exterior.

*bluffing* – Stitching together the canvas and front facings of a coat.

*board* – The long, broad, table-like surface on which a cutter or tailor works, standing or sitting.

*bodkin* – A small plastic pen-shaped tool with a softly pointed tip used for piercing cloth, ripping down basted garments and rounding out the eyelets of hand-worked buttonholes.

*body* – A term applied to textiles, suggesting compactness, solidity and richness of handle in the raw, semi-manufactured or manufactured state.

*body coat* – The term for a coat that hugs the figure with the help of *side bodies* (see below), and that has a waist seam and a skirt. Body coats include frock coats, morning coats and hunt coats.

*bolt* – An entire length of cloth from the loom, rolled or folded. Bolts vary in length.

*bomber jacket* – Also called a 'bombardier' or 'flight' jacket, a type of jacket originally designed in the early twentieth century for use by First World War military pilots, whose cockpits were exposed. Typically made of heavy-duty leather and lined or partially lined with fur, a bomber jacket tends to feature large fold-up or wraparound collars, zip closures with wind flaps, and close-fitting cuffs and waists, all designed to keep the wearer warm. See also pages 140–45.

*Botany* – Originally, Merino wool grown near Botany Bay, Australia; modern usage is to call raw goods 'Merino' and, once they are processed, 'Botany'.

*Botany twill* – A twilled mixture made of Botany wool.

*bouclé* – A novelty yarn and finish effect produced on cloths whereby very small, drawn-out curly loops in the individual threads appear on the surface. The name is from the French *bouclé*, meaning buckle or ringlet.

*bound edge* or *bound seam* – A seam whose fabric edges are bound by thread or lining to prevent fraying or grinning.

*braiding* – A decorative trim typically appearing along the edges of a coat, or down the sides of trousers, and which resembles a plait or braid. Often made of silk.

*breeches* – See *britches*.

*brick stitch* – Stitches resembling brickwork.

*bridle* – A narrow strip of material, usually cotton, added to the canvas inside the lapel in order to hold its roll, as a bridle restrains a horse.

*brilliantine* – Wiry fabric, like alpaca, but of higher lustre, made from Angora goat hair.

*britches* or *breeches* – Calf-length trousers of a durable fabric (such as whipcord, Bedford cord or cavalry twill) flaring at the sides of the thighs and fitting snugly at the knees so as to be worn with boots while hunting or riding. See also *plus-twos* and *plus-fours*.

*broad silk* – Silk a yard (metre) or more wide.

*brocade* – A fabric with decorative woven figures or patterns, often floral. Made on a jacquard loom.

*brushed fabrics* – Cloths with a nap finish.

*buckling* – A fault in weaving because of tight threads and uneven tension.

*buggy lining* – Lining across the back of an otherwise unlined coat – reminiscent of buggy carriages that have an awning but no 'lining' on the front or sides.

*Burberry* – Registered trademark name for weatherproofed cotton garments or fabric.

*button catch* – See *fly catch*.

*button five show six* – A garment (typically a waistcoat) that has six buttons down the front, with the bottom one left undone.

*button stand* – The distance from the finished edge of a garment to the centre of a button.

*buttonhole twist* – The thread used for the stitches around a buttonhole.

*cabbage* – Like mungo, material left over from garment making.

*calico* – A cotton material whose name derives from Calicut, India, where the cloth was first printed with wooden blocks by hand.

*Cambridge grey* – See *Oxford grey*.

*canvas* – A cloth originally made of hemp yarns and with a name derived from the word *cannabis*. Canvas has since come to refer to rough, heavy fabric woven of flax and cotton and sometimes jute. Inserted (and, ideally, hand-stitched) into a coat's collar and chest, it gives a garment its shape and support. Canvas is also used as a verb to describe the assembly of such interfacing.

*car coat* – Originally referred to as 'motoring dress', a type of coat that came into fashion in the early 1900s (that is, with the automobile) and has evolved over the last century to provide protection and warmth to drivers of various styles of vehicles.

*cashmere* – The soft, fine, lightweight, downy yarn and fabric made from the wool at the roots of the hair of the cashmere, or Kashmir, goat.

*catch* – A backing of material providing reinforcement to an opening such as a trouser fly.

*cavalry twill* – A strong cotton, wool or worsted fabric of double twill, with a distinctive diagonal weave, often used to make hunt coats.

*centreline cut* – A style of cutting trousers in which the pattern is drawn using the front pleat line or crease as one's starting and reference point.

*chain stitch* – A flexible, stretchable, ornamental stitch commonly used in the legs and seat seams of trousers. Its thread interloops to look like a chain.

*chalk stripe* – Classic business-suit pattern in which solid, broader-than-pinstripe stripes (i.e., at least ⅛ inch) appear against a contrasting background.

*challis* – A form of crepe, sometimes – and indeed originally – comprising a silk-and-wool blend, but it can can also be made of a single fibre or from synthetic components. The French version tends to be glossy, but many others (including Holland & Sherry's as seen on pages 144–49) have a more matt surface. Challis's name is said to come from the Anglo-Indian word *shallee*, which means 'soft'.

*check* – Term given to a chequerboard appearance produced on a fabric by employing a weave of two or more colours of warp and weft specially arranged. See also *gingham*, *Glen check*, *houndstooth*, *mackinaw*, *pin check*, *Prince of Wales check*, *Tattersall* and *windowpane check*.

*chest piece* – A combination of canvas and felt inserted into the chest of a coat to give it strength and shape.

*chiffon* – A think, gauze-like fabric with a soft or sometimes stiff finish.

*Clapham Junction* – Slang for a pattern draft having several alterations or additions.

*clapper* – An oblong or rectangular piece of hardwood wielded like a paddle to flatten parts of a garment. Also called a 'beater', 'striker' or 'pounding block'.

*clear finish* – See *hard finish*.

*clip* – 1. All of the wool taken from a single flock of sheep. 2. A small, straight cut made into a seam allowance so that the seam will lie flat around curves.

*cocksparrow* – A wing-like effect at the back of a coat.

*collar interfacing* – Stiff, firmly woven linen fabric sewn between a collar's surface and its undercollar.

*corduroy* – A strong, ribbed velveteen fabric made of cotton and whose name comes from the French phrase *corde du roi*, i.e., 'cord of the king'. The material was originally made exclusively to clothe the huntsmen of the Bourbon kings of France.

*counts* – The number of yarns or threads per inch.

*Courtauld crepe* – An extremely popular mourning crepe worn by women in the late nineteenth century. Made by Courtaulds, a UK-based fabric and chemical manufacturer. See also page 45.

*covert coat* – So-named for its colour, which ranges from the brown or fawn to tannish-green of 'covert' thickets inhabited by animals in the woods. Originally designed for hunting and horseback riding, the covert coat is one of the most commonly worn forms of overcoat today. It is usually made of all wool, with the occasional exception of a velvet collar. See also page 147.

*crepe* – A popular fabric made of natural or synthetic fibres twisted and/or treated to give the material's surface a crinkled texture. See also pages 45, 48.

*crimp* – The natural waviness of the wool fibre. It varies with the fibre's diameter.

*Crimplene* – A thick, polyester yarn used to make a wrinkle-resistant 'wash and wear' fabric of the same name. Developed in the mid-1950s by ICI, it was named after the Crimple Valley, where the company was located. See also pages 45–47.

*crooken on* – To bring the fabric of a coat's shoulder closer to the neck point, closing or eliminating the gap visible between the coat and shirt just beside the collar.

*cross-bred* – A term applied to wools obtained from sheep of mixed breed. The bulk of wool manufactured is cross-bred; it is strong, but lacks fineness.

*cross jet* – The small, typically horizontal hem on a coat's inside or outside breast pocket.

*cross pocket* – A horizontal pocket.

*cross stitch* – An ornamental hand stitch that looks like an X.

*crutch* or *crotch* – Point at which the inside leg seams meet. Also *fork*.

*Cupro* – Short for cuprammonium rayon, a synthetic material made from cellulose dissolved in cuprammonium solution and commonly used for garment lining. See also *Bemberg*.

*curtains* – The strips of soft, durable material that hang below a trousers waistband to prevent the waist area from stretching, hold pleats in place and conceal interior stitching. Usually made of the same material used for the waistband, e.g., Ermazine or silk.

*cutter* – The person responsible for measuring the customer, assessing the customer's figuration, cutting a paper pattern and fitting the garment on the customer in its various stages of making, until finished.

*damask* – A figured cloth originally from Damascus.

*dart* – A tapered seam that adjusts the shape and fit of a garment.

*denim* – A coarse twill, today used to make jeans (and other garments, including suits). Its name comes from *de Nîmes*, as in *serges de Nîmes*.

*dice* – Small squares of different colours; a pattern used for the edging of dresses, stockings and tartan for the bands of Highland bonnets.

*dinner jacket* – Often also referred to, especially in American English, as a tuxedo. A formal evening suit, usually in black or midnight blue and embellished with satin or grosgrain facings on the lapels, buttons and down the sides of the accompanying trousers. As part of an ensemble, the dinner jacket satisfied the dress code 'black tie'. See also pages 184–89 and 190–95.

*dogtooth* – A woven fabric pattern reminiscent of canine teeth. See also *houndstooth*.

*Donegal* (or *donegal*) *tweed* – A coarse, plain or herringbone tweed with coloured slubs, i.e., flecks, that traditionally comes from County Donegal, Ireland, but now exists in Scottish and Italian versions called *donegal*.

*double-breasted* – Term to describe a coat, jacket or similar garment having two parallel columns of buttons, a wide overlap of fabric and a more formal, peaked lapel.

*dressing gown* – A more elegant and socially presentable form of the bathrobe, commonly worn by men in days of yore. See also pages 68–71.

*duffel* (or *duffle*) *coat* – A coat made of a thick woollen material that hails from the small town of Duffel, in the Antwerp province of Belgium. The original British style would be knee-length or shorter and made of a genuine double-weave duffel, with three or four toggles in wood or horn running down the front and fastened by a piece of leather or rope.

*dupion silk* – A lustrous silk often woven from two different colours of threads, so that the fabric shimmers or changes colour in the light.

# E

*ease* – An even distribution of fullness in fabric, created without perceptible gathers or tucks.

*Ermazine* – A light, well-ventilated lining alternative to silk, typically used in fancier coats.

*Estrato* – A stretchable worsted fabric woven from Merino wool and created by Trabaldo Togna, an Italian mill in Biella, to be flexible and wrinkle-resistant.

# F

*facing* – A garment's covering or lining in places such as the silk lapels on a tailcoat.

*fawn* – A light yellowish-brown colour.

*fell* – To sew or finish a seam with the raw edges flattened, turned under and stitched down.

*figuration* – A bespoke cutter's notes on a customer's physique, particularly any bodily idiosyncrasies – such as a stoop, a paunch, arms of dissimilar length or uneven shoulder blades – that affect how a garment hangs. The bespoke cutter uses these observations (along with his Rock of Eye) to individualize the customer's pattern so that it both fits precisely and is maximally flattering. See also pages 29–31.

*findings* – Padding and interfacing materials used to reinforce and structure a garment.

*finishes* – Finished coats, ready for a final fitting and, provided the customer is satisfied, removal from the shop.

*fishtail* – On the back of a pair of trousers requiring braces, the slightly higher cut tab with a V-shaped opening to which braces are attached and which resembles a fish's tail.

*fitting* – One of the two, three or more stages in the making of a suit or other bespoke or custom-made garment during which it is donned by the customer and assessed by customer and cutter together for necessary adjustments.

*flannel* – A soft and slightly napped fabric of wool or cotton combination, usually used for the making up of suits. Probably a variant on the Middle English *flanyn*, or sackcloth; in turn from the Old French *flaine*, for a coarse kind of wool.

*flash basting* – Superfluous basting stitches that are put into a garment at the fitting stage (or for display in a shop window or website photograph) to impress the customer.

*float* – Excess material, e.g., approximately ⅛ inch of surplus where the sleeve of a coat meets the scye.

*floating canvas* – The canvas inside a hand-canvassed coat. It 'floats' between the facing and forepart rather than being adhered into place by chemical means.

*fly* – An inner flap on trousers, an overcoat, or indeed any other garment to conceal a row of buttons or zip. In trousers the fly is on the crutch opening in front of the left side and is stitched on to conceal the method of fastening. It is made up and has buttonholes worked into it before being fastened onto the left topside.

*fly catch* (or *button catch*) – The counterpart of the fly, seamed onto the right topside. The buttons on the catch are what fasten the fly parts together.

*flyline* – The line up the centre of the front of the trousers from the seat to the waistband.

*flyline cut* – A style of cutting trousers in which the pattern is drawn using the fly as a starting and reference point.

*football buttons* – Buttons that resemble semispherical truncated icosahedrons, otherwise known as footballs (or soccer balls, in American terminology), in brown leather.

*fork* – The point on a pair of trousers where the legs join. Also *crutch* or *crotch*.

*forward* (or *advance*) *fitting* – The second or subsequent stage of a garment's assembly, after it has already been basted, fitted once on the customer, and ripped down and re-cut if necessary according to the adjusted pattern.

*French tack* – A chain of thread that connects the hem of a lining to the garment hem.

*fresco* – A cool, well-ventilated, high-quality plain-weave worsted fabric patented in 1907 by English manufacturer Huddersfield especially for the making up of business suits and other necessary clothing worn in hot climates.

*frock coat* – A standard form of dress during the Victorian and Edwardian eras and distinguished by its 'skirt', which goes all the way around the wearer's legs just above or at the knee. See also *body coat* and pages 160–65.

*fusing* – A method of securing canvas in place in the collars and chests of coats using chemicals whose adhesive qualities are awakened at high temperatures. Fusing is a cheaper and less time-consuming method of securing canvas, but it does not last as long as comprehensive hand-stitching and can lead to a corrugated appearance over time, especially if the garment in question is treated repeatedly to dry-cleaning.

*fustian* – A thick and durable twilled cotton cloth with a short nap, usually dyed in dark colours. As fustian was often used for padding, the word is also used to describe speech or writing thought to be pompous or overdone – i.e., padded.

# G

*gabardine* – A sturdy, smooth-finish fabric of worsted, cotton, polyester or other fibre, with a tight twill weave and fairly resistant to creasing. It is most often used to make up trousers and blazers. See also pages 50–55.

*gimp* – Heavy cord made of silk, cotton or wool strands with a wire core, used to reinforce the edges of hand-worked buttonholes.

*gingham* – A yarn-dyed, plain-weave fabric with a pattern of stripes or checks. The name is thought to have come into English usage from the Dutch *gingang*, which in turn is supposed to have come from the Malay *genggang*, which means 'ajar' or 'with space between' – like the spaces between stripes or checks.

*Glen check* (also *Glen plaid* or *Glenurquhart plaid*) – A classic plaid pattern of muted colours or black and grey or white, often with two dark and two light stripes alternating with four dark and four light stripes, horizontally and vertically, forming a crisscross pattern of irregular checks. Named after Glen Urquhart in Invernesshire, Scotland. See also *Prince of Wales check*.

*The Glorious Twelfth* – 12 August, i.e., the official start of grouse-shooting season.

*gorge line* – Line made by a diagonal seam joining the collar end to the lapel top.

*grain* – The direction of threads in a woven fabric. The warp forms the lengthwise grain while the weft forms the crosswise grain.

*grinning* – The straining or pulling apart at the seams of fabric that has not been sufficiently reinforced.

*grosgrain* – In American English, the term for ribbed, or corded material.

*Guanashina* – A rare, specially commissioned blend of the three finest fibres in the world: Andean guanaco, pashmina and yearling cashmere.

# H

*haircloth* – A wiry, resilient interfacing fabric made from a mixture of strong cotton fibres and horsehair.

*ham* – A firm, ham-shaped cushion with built-in curves that conform to various contours of the body and which is used for pressing garment areas that need special shaping.

*handle* – The feel of a fabric. See also *texture*.

*hard finish* or *clear finish* – The surface of a fabric that has no nap, either naturally or because the nap has been sheared off.

*Harrington jacket* – Basically a lighter-weight version of the *bomber jacket* (see above) in cotton, wool, nylon, polyester or thin leather. First introduced by Baracuta and Grenfell in the 1930s, it was nicknamed the 'Harrington jacket' because Ryan O'Neal donned a Baracuta G9 while playing Rodney Harrington in *Peyton Place*.

*Harris tweed* – Heavy, hairy, hand-woven tweed from the Outer Hebrides.

*herringbone* – Worsted fabric with a chevron pattern, most often used to make up suits and overcoats.

*hickory stripe* – A relatively heavy, navy-and-white striped fabric once popular in the American West for making up the overalls, jackets and caps worn by railroad engineers (and still manufactured today by the workclothes supplier Dickies).

*hopsack* – Coarse, loosely woven cotton, wool or jute-like fibres whose texture resembles that of burlap.

*horsehair canvas* – One of the types of canvas used in building the inner construction of a coat, to give the chest and upper forepart shape and support.

*houndstooth* – A distinctive tessellated check pattern comprising what look like tiny lightning bolts, or jagged canine teeth. Generally two different colours of thread are woven together in equal measure, so there is no dominant background or foreground colour; when the colours are very contrasting, the pattern is very dramatic. A common choice for sporting garments.

*hunt buttons* – Buttons engraved with the insignia of a specific hunt and, once 'earned', worn on a participant's coat and vest as part of the hunt uniform.

*hunter's pink* – The standard colour, a vivid scarlet, that melton intended for frock and dress coats for riding with hounds is dyed.

# I

*inauguration cloth* – A heavyweight, superfine black and unfinished twill worsted fabric for double-breasted frock and morning coats. Named as such in honour of US President McKinley's 1897 inauguration suit.

*inbreast* – A pocket on the inside breast of a coat.

*ICI* – Imperial Chemical Industries PLC. Formed in 1926 from the merger of four British chemical companies. Now part of AkzoNobel, a leading chemical supplier and coatings manufacturer.

*indigo* – A vegetable substance extracted from the leaves and stems of certain tropical and semi-tropical plants and from which brilliant and durable blue dyes are obtained.

*interfacing* – Fabric sewn between two layers of garment fabric to stiffen and strengthen different parts of the garment.

*interlining* – An inner lining placed between the lining and outer fabric of a garment for extra warmth or bulk.

# J

*jacket* – A short coat whose name supposedly originated with the French name Jacques, a common nickname for a male peasant.

*jacketing* – Fabric for jackets or coats.

*Jacquard* – A simple method of weaving intricate designs into fabric, invented by the Frenchman Joseph Marie Jacquard.

*jeans* – The common term for denim trousers, said to come from the French name for Genoa, *Gênes*, whose sailors typically wore clothes of the same indigo hue.

*jetted pocket* – A pocket that does not have a flap. Unlike a patch pocket, and also a welted pocket, the only part of a jetted pocket that's visible is its opening, which is typically edged with *jetting* (see below). The most formal kind of pocket.

*jetting* – A small strip of leather or fabric, such as satin, sewn along the edge of a jetted pocket.

*jigger button* – The button placed inside the left forepart of a man's double-breasted coat or waistcoat to keep the underneath forepart in position.

# K

*keyhole buttonhole* – A buttonhole with one rounded end, such that it looks like a keyhole. This is often an indication that the buttonhole is machine-made, and therefore can give the impression of inferior quality.

*keyhole lapel* – A lapel with a keyhole buttonhole.

*khaki* – A light yellow-brownish colour whose name derives from the Persian *khâk*, which means 'soil'.

*kimono* – A loose robe with wide sleeves and a sash around the waist, usually associated with Japanese garb. The name comes from the Japanese words for 'wear' (*ki*) and 'thing' (*mono*).

*kink* – A snarl or curl produced by a hard-twisted thread receding upon itself.

*knickerbocker yarns* – Yarns spotted or striped, usually in several colours.

*knitting* – The process of making fabric by interlocking series of loops or one or more yarns.

*knot* – 1. A fault in a cloth, caused by the joining of broken warp or weft. 2. A snugly looped tie.

# L

*lamb's wool* – A fine yarn composed of the fine wool shorn from young sheep in their first year.

*lanolin* – The wax secreted by wool-growing animals. Its name comes from the Latin *lana*, for wool, and *oleum*, for oil.

*lapthair* – A type of canvas inserted in the chest area of a coat to give it body and shape.

*laventine* – A very thin silk fabric usually used to line sleeves.

*lightweights* – Lightweight fabrics, such as an 8- or 9-ounce (227–255 gram) mohair, used for clothing to be worn in warm climates or interiors.

*linen* – Fabric and yarn made of flax fibres.

*list* – The edge or selvedge of a piece.

*listed* – A defect in the list or edge of a garment, such as the edge being torn away, stained or frayed.

*Liverpool pocket* – A ticket pocket with a welt inside. See also *welt pocket*.

*llama* – A South American mountain animal resembling the camel, but smaller. Cloth made with an admixture of the animal's soft, furry hair is quite luxurious and often used for formalwear.

*lookbook* – A collection or portfolio of photographs or other images assembled to exhibit a model, photographer, style, stylist or clothing line.

*lounge coat* – The term for the modern coat or jacket that comprises the top half of a suit.

*lovat* – A greyish colour that also incorporates other shades, especially green, and is common among sporting fabrics and plaids. Its name is thought to be after Thomas Alexander Fraser, Lord Lovat (1802–1875), who promoted the wearing of tweeds in muted colours as hunting dress.

# M

*mackinaw* – Coarse heavyweight fabric with a large check pattern of many colours and usually used to make the topcoats or belted jackets of the same name. Once popular among North American lumberjacks.

*madder* – A Eurasian plant whose root supplies a red pigment used to dye wool and other fabrics.

*made-to-measure* – The term used to describe a garment made according to the customer's measurements (and sometimes with cloth chosen by the customer) but which is then cut and assembled in a factory according to standard block patterns and then adjusted. A less individualized (and therefore less expensive) alternative to a true and traditionally made bespoke suit.

*madras* – A type of soft fabric (muslin) usually with fancy patterns used in shirting.

*mandarin collar* (or *stand collar*) – A short stand-up collar that evokes those associated with mandarins in Imperial China. See also Nehru coat, and pages 178–83.

*melton* – A heavily milled woollen in which the fibres have been made to stand straight up and then the piece cut bare to conceal the weave. Made with a cotton warp and a woollen weft. Used for overcoats, hunting jackets, etc., particularly on the underside of collars. Named for the town Melton Mowbray, England.

*Merino wool* – The best (softest and lightest) quality wool from sheep originally bred in Spain; used for suits.

*micro* – Microlite fabric, which is 70% wool, 30% microfibre. It is a lightweight alternative to 100% natural fabrics, good for hot climates.

*micron* – The unit of measurement used for wool fibre diameter. One micron = 1 millionth of a metre.

*mohair* – The fine, soft, silky hair of the angora goat. It has a slight sheen, is crease-resistant and ideal for summer suits and dresswear. Imitation mohair made of wool and cotton combinations is detectable because its fibres cling closely together, whereas the fibres of mohair are clearly separable.

*moleskin* – Sturdy and heavily napped twilled cotton fabric that resembles the skin of a mole and is often used for casual, sport and working trousers.

*mood board* – A type of collage that artists and designers use to get a flavour of how different aesthetic elements work together.

*morning coat* – A tailcoat typically made of black herringbone fabric and worn at formal events such as weddings and races such as Ascot.

*mounting* – A tightly woven fabric cut in the shapes of the main pieces of a garment and attached to these pieces before the garment is sewn together. Used usually for women's garments.

*Moygashel* – A brand name that for many years was synonymous with high-quality Irish linen that has very beautiful natural slubs and creases.

*mungo* – Material remnants too small or inferior in quality to be used for garment-making and which cutters and tailors use to practise technique or as rags. The word also once referred to longer lengths of fabric made up of the smaller remnants, which tailors would bring to shops that specialized in recycling them.

*muslin* – An inexpensive, plain-woven cotton fabric used for making prototypes of garments as an aid to styling and fitting.

# N

*nailhead* – A subtle geometric fabric pattern wherein a solid background colour is offset by many small nailhead-sized depressions at regular and very small intervals. The background colour tends to dominate, but the nailheads' colour can be brought out with a tie or shirt of the same colour.

*nap* – A fabric's short surface fibres that have been drawn out and brushed in one direction, such as on velvet or corduroy.

*natural waist* – The torso circumference where it intersects with the small of the back. Positioning the front button on a single-breasted coat at the natural waist will have the optical effect of thinning and elongating the wearer's figure.

*Nehru coat* – A coat inspired by the Indian *achkan* or *sherwani* garments frequently worn by Jawaharlal Nehru, prime minister of India from 1947 until 1964. Nehru coats vary in length, fabric, and type and number of fasteners, but all feature the same distinctive *mandarin collar* (see above). See also pages 178–83.

*Newmarket coat* – A long body coat worn in the nineteenth century, usually as a riding coat by men and as an overcoat by women. Its name would seem to come from the town of Newmarket, Suffolk, generally considered to be the birthplace of thoroughbred horseracing.

*noble* – A general term for fine wool and other luxury animal fibres, e.g., mohair, alpaca, vicuña.

*Norfolk coat* or *jacket* – A loose, belted single-breasted coat with box pleats for a gun and cartridges; worn in the country for game shooting.

*notch* – A V- or diamond-shaped mark made on the edge of a garment piece as an alignment guide. Also a triangular cut into the seam allowance to help it to lie flat.

*notched lapel* (or *step lapel*) – A lapel sewn to the collar at an angle, such that the junction looks like a step. Notched lapels are standard on single-breasted suits, blazers and sport coats. The size of the notch varies; a small notch is called a fishmouth.

*nothing at the neck point* – The point on a shoulder immediately next to the collar. 'Nothing' refers to the distance away from the collar or neck point.

*nothing at the top* – The point on a line or seam immediately next to its top. 'Nothing' refers to the distance away from the top of the line or seam.

*notions* – Items such as buttons, hooks and zips required to finish a garment.

*nylon* – A synthetic material with a chemical composition akin to that of proteins (e.g., silk, hair and wool) but which has no exact counterpart in nature.

*off-the-peg* – Made in standard sizes and available from merchandise in stock. Synonymous with 'ready-to-wear'.

*on the back seam* – An elegant euphemism for 'on one's backside', as in, 'to fall on one's back seam.' Also to lie down on one's tailoring board for a short siesta.

*on the double* – On both the front and back.

*operation* – A patch, especially on the trousers' seat.

*outbreast* – A pocket on the outside breast of a coat.

*overcheck* and *overplaid* – A pattern effect made by the superimposition of one check over another check; often seen in the tartans of Scottish clans.

*Oxford grey* – A dark grey fabric made of mixed dyed black and white wools. A lighter version is called 'Cambridge grey', a distinction corresponding to the two universities' colours: Oxford's is dark blue while Cambridge's is light blue.

*Oxfords* (and *pinpoint Oxfords*) – A style of leather shoe with enclosed lacing and which originally appeared in Scotland and Ireland, where they are occasionally called Balmorals. Oxfords with ornamental pinpoint-like perforations in the leather are pinpoint Oxfords.

*padding* – A stitch or addition of materials to an area of a garment to give it shape.

*paisley* – Patterns reminiscent of those in shawls originally made in the Scottish town of Paisley.

*pashmina* – A luxurious soft wool from the pashmina goat, bred in northern India and commonly found in the high-altitude deserts of Tibet and Kashmir.

*pass a coat* – What a cutter does to check whether a coat is progressing well and properly in the making-up process. He puts the coat on himself (or a fellow employee, if the coat is too small for his own frame) and scrutinizes its reflection in a mirror to confirm that in every last respect it meets his standards before it proceeds to be fitted on the customer or dispatched.

*pass up* – To rip open the side seams and move the back panel up to create more length in the back.

*patch pocket* – A pocket made of a separate piece of cloth sewn onto the outside of a garment.

*pea coat* – A short, double-breasted overcoat of coarse woollen cloth, based on a style originally associated with mariners and American and British naval uniforms. See also pages 122–27.

*peaked lapel* – The most formal style of lapel, which peaks upward at the junction of lapel and collar. Peaked lapels are standard on double-breasted jackets and formal coats including tailcoats and morning coats.

*pencil stripe* – Akin to pinstripes, an effect on cloths whereby contrasting threads are woven in lines suggestive of having been drawn on by a pencil.

*pheasant-eye spot* – Like a birdseye pattern, but with larger 'eyes'.

*pick-and-pick* – Textured plain cloth made up of single filling threads in different colours. Also called 'sharkskin'.

*pile* – A fabric having a surface made of upright ends, as in fur.

*pin check* – An effect on suiting material, often in grey and white, where the small checks of the pattern are a size almost that of a pinhead.

*pinstripes* – The classic English suit fabric distinguished by its very thin stripes. The lines in 'true' pinstripes are solid lines; 'rain pinstripes' comprise tiny unjoined dots; and 'cable' pinstripes look like tiny braids.

*piping* – A narrowly folded strip of garment fabric usually used to finish the top and bottom edges of a pocket opening.

*plaid* – Fabric with the checked and lined pattern of Scottish tartan cloth.

*plain weave* – A weave in which the yarns are interlaced in a simple chequerboard fashion.

*pleat* – A crisp fold (like those in an accordion's bellows) incorporated into a garment that allows the garment to expand when the wearer makes certain gestures or movements.

*plugging* – Fastening purely ornamental buttons onto fabric by forcing the button's shank through the cloth and securing it on the other side with a plug of linen or other material so the button lies flat against the garment.

*plus-twos* – Three-quarter-length trousers that buckle under the knee (technically 2 inches below the knee) to look like baggy breeches and which are typically worn when hunting or shooting.

*plus-fours* – Slightly longer than three-quarter-length trousers that buckle under the knee (technically 4 inches below the knee) to look like baggy breeches and which are typically worn when hunting or shooting.

*plys* – 1. Layers of cloth. 2. The strands twisted together to make yarn, rope or thread.

*poacher's pocket* – A large interior pocket named for the practice of hiding felled game or other shooting victims in order to 'poach' one's conquest off the field. A poacher's pocket is prevented from visibly weighing down a coat by a strip of fabric that suspends the pocket in place. See also pages 110–13.

*pocketing fabric* – Silk or tightly woven twilled cotton fabric with a satiny finish and which is used to line pockets.

*poplin* – A finely corded fabric made of cotton, rayon, silk or wool; named for *papelino*, that is, coming originally from Avignon, famed for its papal residence.

*pre-shrink* – To shrink fabric to an irreducible degree before cutting it.

*press mitt* – A thumbless padded mitten used to press small curved areas that do not fit over a tailor's ham or regular ironing board.

*presser foot* – The part of a sewing machine that holds down fabric while it advances under the needle.

*pressing cloth* – A piece of fabric, usually cotton, placed between the iron and garment while pressing.

*Prince of Wales check* – An alternative term for *Glen* or *Glenurquhart* check. Popularized by the Duke of Windsor when he was Prince of Wales, but reputedly originally designed by King Edward VII when he was Prince of Wales.

*puff cut* – A short cut made in the canvas inserted in the breast panels of a coat to prevent the outer material from stringing.

*pyjamas* – Sleeping clothes whose name is said to come from the Persian for 'leg clothing'.

# R

*raglan sleeve* – A sleeve whose seams slant outward from neck to underarm, dispensing with the vertical shoulder seam on a 'normal' jacket and allowing for more freedom of movement. Named after Baron Raglan, who lost an arm during the Battle of Waterloo and thereafter wore a raglan sleeve to accommodate his stump.

*rain pinstripes* – Pinstripes comprising tiny unjoined dots that appear to be 'raining' down the material.

*ranter* – To sew a seam such that it is invisible, or nearly so.

*ratcatcher* – A relatively informal fox-hunting coat or ensemble, such as a tweed jacket and tan riding breeches, worn on non-hunt days or by unofficial or junior-ranking participants in a hunt.

*raw edged* – An edge that has not been hemmed or turned in. Only practicable with meltons and other materials that do not fray or unravel.

*ready-to-wear* – Made in standard sizes and available from merchandise in stock. Synonymous with 'off-the-peg'.

*regatta stripe* – Lightweight or woollen suiting (e.g., flannel) with a neat fancy stripe effect.

*reinforce* – To strengthen a seam with additional stitches or to add an extra layer of fabric to a stress area.

*rip down* – The removal, typically using a bodkin, of the stitches from a basted garment so that it can be adjusted and reassembled more formally.

*Rock of Eye* – The faculty that allows a cutter to draw and cut a pattern practically freehand, unguided except by basic measurements and the cutter's cultivated instinct that it 'looks right' and will accommodate the customer's figuration in the most comfortable yet flattering way. See pages 29–31.

*roebuck suede* – Skin of the male roe deer.

*roll collar* – See *shawl lapel*.

*roll line* – The pattern marking along which the collar and lapel are turned back.

*roped* – Describes a sleeve that has been attached too high on the armhole of a coat and therefore puffs up at the shoulder.

# S

saddle stitch – A running stitch typically set in slightly from a garment's edge and used as much (or exclusively) for decorative purposes as for joining. Common on clothing and also leather articles, such as saddles, from whence it gets its name.

safari coat – A garment originally designed to be worn on safari in the African bush. Typically made of a lightweight and relatively aerated material in a khaki colour, the safari coat tends to feature a belt, epaulette-like shoulder straps called passants, and bellows pockets. Also called a 'safari jacket' or 'bush jacket' – or, when paired with trousers, a 'safari suit'. See also pages 62–67.

satin – A warp or weft surface cloth in which the intersections of warp and weft are so arranged as to be imperceptible.

Savile Row Bespoke Association – An association established in 2004 to protect and develop the craft of bespoke tailoring as well as its continued residence on Savile Row and its Mayfair surrounds. At writing, members include: Alexander McQueen; Anderson & Sheppard; Chittleborough & Morgan; Davies & Son; Dege & Skinner; Gieves & Hawkes; H. Huntsman & Sons; Hardy Amies; Henry Poole & Co.; Kent, Haste & Lachter; Kilgour; Meyer & Mortimer; Norton & Sons; Richard Anderson; Richard James; and Welsh & Jefferies.

Saxony – High-grade wool, yarn and worsted cloth produced from the Merino sheep of Saxony.

scale, tailoring – A wooden device, marked with fractions to identify relative dimensions and ratios of reduction or enlargement, which is used in the drawing of patterns.

scroop – The feel associated with silk and given to rayon and other synthetic sateens by chemical means.

scye – A contraction of the words 'arm's' and 'eye', a scye is the round opening in a coat into which a sleeve is inserted. The 'depth of scye' measurement is the distance from the armpit to the shoulder line.

seam – A line of junction between two edges.

seam allowance – The fabric that extends outside a seam line.

seat allowance – The quantity allowed for expansion of a trousers' seat when the wearer is seated.

seconds – Pieces of cloth containing visible faults.

seersucker – A lightweight fabric with crinkled stripes that may be laundered without ironing. Its name derives from the Persian words for 'milk' (shir) and 'sugar' (shakar), allegedly because the smoothness of milk and the granularity of sugar bear some resemblance to the material's alternating textures.

selvedge – The narrow, lengthwise finished edge of a woven fabric that prevents it from unravelling.

serge – Term for all fabrics of a twill character and of a rough make, distinguished from the finer make of worsteds.

shading – An optical effect produced by different colours or qualities of material or weave in combination,

e.g., an illusion of darkening caused by the misalignment of pieces of patterned (usually checked) cloth.

shadow stripe – A stripe pattern wherein the stripe has only a very subtle difference in texture or shade from the background colour (e.g., medium grey on dark grey). Shadow stripes are generally solid lines, as opposed to cable or rain pinstripes.

shank – The link of buttonhole twist (thread) between a button and the fabric onto which it is sewn, or the small pillar on a button to be fastened to a garment by plugging.

sharkskin – See pick-and-pick.

shawl lapel (also called a roll or shawl collar) – A lapel with a continuous curve. Original to the Victorian smoking jacket, shawl lapels are now given occasionally to dinner jackets and tuxedos in which a slightly less formal look is desired.

shearling – The short wool or skin of a yearling sheep that has been shorn only once.

Shetland tweed – A rich, loose, porous tweed woven from sheep raised on the Shetland Islands, an archipelago north of Scotland.

shirting – Cloth recognized as being suitable for the making up of shirts.

shuttle loom – A loom that weaves material using a continuous cross-thread (the weft) that is passed on a shuttle back and forth along the length of the bolt.

side bodies – Rounded panels on the back of a body coat that give the garment added shape into the small of the back and through the waist at the side seam.

side seam – The seam that runs down the side of a garment.

silesia – A lightweight, smoothly finished, twilled cotton for garment linings, e.g., in coat pockets.

silk – The filaments created by the silkworm in spinning its cocoon.

single-breasted – Term to describe a coat, jacket or similar garment having one column of buttons and a narrow overlap of fabric. The single-breasted style of coat tends to slim and elongate the wearer's appearance.

single-stitch – The clear, single stitch that appears along the edges of a coat, e.g., on the lapels. In the case of tweed garments this stitched area would be slightly 'swelled', i.e., set in slightly to create a wider margin, just for style.

sizing – A finishing process in which a substance (e.g., glue or starch) is added to the yarn and cloth to give it additional strength, stiffness, smoothness or to increase its weight.

skein – A strand of yarn or thread wound around a spool in a series of crossings.

slanted patch pockets – Pockets external to the body of a garment or accessory and patched on at an angle to the garment's centre line.

sleeve caps – Strips of cotton wadding or lamb's wool fleece placed around the tops of sleeves to create a smooth line and to support the roll at the sleeve top.

sleeve cushion – A long, flat pad with a sleeve-like silhouette that is inserted into a completed sleeve during pressing to prevent wrinkling and unwanted creases.

*slub* – A slight irregularity in yarn or fabric achieved either accidentally or intentionally by knotting or twisting, or by including uneven lengths of the fibre when spinning.

*soft finish* – A fuzzy nap on the surface of a fabric. The nap may be natural or created artificially by brushing a smooth fabric with steel combs.

*sport coat* – Typically a single-breasted patterned jacket worn with contrasting trousers.

*staghorn* – A piece of a stag's antler, which can be used for buttons or other decorative elements.

*stand collar* – See *mandarin collar*.

*stay* – An extra piece of fabric sewn into a garment to reinforce a point of possible wear, such as a crutch, heel or trouser pocket.

*stay stitch* – A line of regular machine stitches, sewn along the seam line of a garment piece before the seam is stitched.

*step lapel* – See *notched lapel*.

*strike* – To cut cloth.

*stringing* – Undesirable pleating or creasing in fabric, usually between the shoulder and breast.

*suit* – A three-piece outfit consisting of a matching coat, trousers and waistcoat.

*suiting* – Fabric for suits.

*super 100s/120s/150s* – Types of cloth whose numbers refer to the maximum worsted count of yarn to which that particular type of wool can be spun. The higher the number, the finer the cloth.

*swatch* – A strip or square of cloth, loose or bound in a swatch book, used for sampling.

*syddo* – See *tropical syddo*.

*synthetic* – Man-made, as in material produced from chemical elements, treatment or compounds.

# T

*tack* – Several stitches made in the same place to reinforce a point of strain or to hold garment parts permanently in position.

*taffeta* – A plain, closely woven, smooth, crisp fabric. Originally a rich silk used in England in the seventeenth century.

*tailcoat* – A man's fitted coat, usually black, cut away at the hips and descending in a pair of tapering skirts behind. Tailcoats tend to have silk facings and covered buttons and are worn to white-tie events.

*tailor* – The general term for an artisan who works at a tailoring house. Although referring not to a cutter but to a worker who assembles the cut cloth, the word comes from the French *tailler*, 'to cut'.

*tartan* – An old name for plain woollen army wear, as well as for the distinctive checks-and-lines patterns associated with the Highland clans of Scotland.

*Tattersall* – A check or plaid pattern often comprising two alternating colours, typically a darker stripe against a light background, named for Tattersall's horse market in London where horse blankets with the pattern were sold.

*terrycloth* – A pile fabric, usually made of cotton, with small loops covering its surface, as on a Turkish towel.

*texture* (or *handle*) – The surface effect of cloth.

*thornproof tweed* – Tweed with a tighter, higher-twist weave that makes it less easily puncturable by thorns and branches. See also pages 103 and 108.

*ticket pocket* or *ticket right cross* – A small subpocket (to accommodate tickets, traditionally) usually found inside the right outside breast pocket on a coat.

*toggle* – A rod-shaped button that is inserted into a large buttonhole, loop or frog to fasten a garment. Used especially on sports clothes and outerwear.

*toile* – A basted-together 'draft' or trial run of a garment, usually in a less expensive (and therefore disposable) fabric than the one chosen.

*top-stitching* – A line of machine stitching on the visible side of the garment parallel to a seam.

*trim* – To cut away excess fabric in a seam allowance after a seam has been stitched.

*trimmings* – The accessories required for the making and ornamenting of any article of dress: canvas, silk, buttons, buttonhole twist, etc.

*tropical syddo* – Canvas inserted in the length of the front of a jacket to give it body and shape.

*trouser curtain* – See *curtains*.

*trousering* – Cloth recognized as suitable for making up into trousers.

*tulle* – A fine lace-net fabric, one of the first such man-made materials.

*turn-ups* (or *upturn*) – Hems, or rather cuffs on the bottom of trouser legs, usually 1⅝ inches deep and referred to as 'PTUs', 'Permanent Turn-Ups.'

*tuxedo* – American term for a long-tailed dinner jacket said to have been conceived originally by Henry Poole's on Savile Row for Pierre Lorillard, whose son Griswold first wore it in 1886 to the Tuxedo Park country club in New York. See also *dinner jacket*.

*tweed* – Woollen goods, plain or twilled, felted or rough-finished, woven with dyed yarns and typically made into suits, skirts and overcoats. Originally tweeds were twilled cloths woven of Cheviot wool with a heavy nap, but the name is now applied to many woollen cloths of a light make, including Harris tweeds, Irish Donegal, handwoven tweeds, fancy tweeds and an almost infinite variety of colours and patterns.

*twill weave* – A fundamental weave admitting of many variations, including serge and denim, and in which the intersection of yarn forms lines running to the right or left diagonally across the fabric.

*twist* – An alternative term for thread, or the number of yarns about its axis per unit of length of a yarn or other textile strand. Twist is expressed in turns per inch (tpi), turns per metre (tpm), or turns per centimetre (tpcm).

# U

*undercollar* – The part of the coat collar one sees when one lifts the collar up.

*undercollar fabric* – The fabric that is sewn to the collar interfacing to form the underside of the collar. In women's clothing, it is often of the same fabric as the rest of the garment. In men's, it is typically melton in a colour complementary to the rest of the coat.

*upturn* – See *turn-ups*.

*Velcro* – The brand name of a popular two-ply, self-adhesive hook-and-loop fabric invented by a huntsman and Swiss engineer, George de Mestral, in 1948, inspired by burdock burrs he encountered in the Alps. The word *Velcro* is a portmanteau of the French words *velours* ('velvet') and *crochet* ('hook').

*vent* – The slits or openings in the back of a coat between its tail flaps that allow its hemline to move when the wearer bends or reaches into a trouser pocket.

*vest* – The correct term for a waistcoat, always worn with a suit until after the Second World War.

*vicuña* – The South American vicuña (a camelid relative of the guanaco, but smaller), inhabiting the higher regions of Bolivia and Chile. Its long, silky hair is of the highest textile quality and when first used was made into fine broadcloth, but as the vicuña has become endangered its wool is now extremely rare.

*voile* – Lightweight, semi-sheer fabric of wool, silk, rayon or cotton constructed in plain weave.

*Vulcanite* – A type of rubber that has been vulcanized, i.e., treated with sulfur so that it becomes more durable and elastic. Often used to make combs and buttons, such as the buttons on a hunt coat before its owner has earned official hunt buttons.

*wadding* – Shoulder pads, often in a grey, multi-flecked felt-like substance cut into a half-moon and shaped into plys, with collar canvas inserted for strength.

*waistband interfacing* – A strip of strong, canvas-like fabric used for reinforcement around the waist.

*waistcoat* – A vest that may be worn with or without the other two components of a suit.

*warp* – Threads running lengthwise in a piece of cloth.

*weave* – The interlacing of warp and weft.

*weft* – Threads running crosswise in a piece of cloth.

*welt* – Strips of cloth or other reinforcements sewn or otherwise fastened to an edge, pocket or border of a garment to strengthen or adorn it.

*welt pocket* (or *Liverpool pocket*) – An interior pocket that opens to the outside, finished with a horizontal band of garment fabric that covers the opening.

*whipcord* – Hard-wearing cotton, woollen or worsted fabric with a steep, diagonally ribbed surface, similar to cavalry twill; used for trousers and military uniforms.

*windowpane check* – A check pattern in which the checks are quite large.

*woad* – A European plant belonging to the mustard family and whose leaves contain a blue pigment that is extracted for the purpose of dyeing fibres and fabric.

*wool* – The hair from sheep, lamb and certain other animals which is spun, woven, knitted or felted into fabric for clothing.

*woollen* – Fabric made from short, uncombed fibres of wool, characteristically soft to the touch and often finished with a nap. Woollen fibres are not parallel but crossed in what appears to be a haphazard arrangement. Not necessarily synonymous with 'all-wool'.

*worsted* – Clear, smooth-handled fabric in which the structure and colour are well-defined owing to the smoothness of its yarns and interlacing. Gabardine and serge are worsteds.

*wrap* – The extent to which the two front halves of an overcoat overlap.

*yarn* – Natural or synthethic spun fibres that can be woven into fabric.

*yeddo* – A soft, medium-weight cotton crepe popular in England in the late nineteenth century and which takes its name from the former name of Tokyo.

*zephyr* – A fine, light cotton fabric generally woven with dyed yarns in a variety of fancy patterns.

# ACKNOWLEDGMENTS

Thanks must firstly go to Lucas Dietrich and his fine team at Thames & Hudson Ltd, London: in particular, the diligent Flora Spiegel, Fleur Jones and Jane Cutter.

To Lisa Halliday for her enthusiasm, professionalism and friendship throughout – it's been a pleasure to work with you again.

To Fran Anderson for her beautiful sketches and dedication.

To Stu Smith, our art director par excellence, and to Allon Kaye and Justine Schuster, the book's designers.

Also to Brian Lishak for his continuous wise counsel, and to all the colleagues, friends and customers who cross the threshold here at No. 13 Savile Row to make, wear and enjoy beautiful clothes.

# PICTURE CREDITS

**About the Author**

Master cutter Richard Anderson has worked on Savile Row for over thirty-five years. He started his career at the age of seventeen as an apprentice at Huntsman. In 2001 he co-founded his own Savile Row company, Richard Anderson Ltd, with Brian Lishak. His memoir *Bespoke: Savile Row Ripped and Smoothed* was published to great acclaim in 2009.

**To Tony and Alice**

On the cover: Details of Richard Anderson jackets; all cover images courtesy Richard Anderson

First published in the United Kingdom in 2018 by Thames & Hudson Ltd, 181A High Holborn, London WC1V 7QX

Designed by SMITH;
Allon Kaye and Justine Schuster
www.smithdesign.com

British Library Cataloguing-in-Publication Data

A catalogue record for this book is available from the British Library

ISBN 978-0-500-02149-1

Printed and bound in China by Toppan Leefung Printing Limited

To find out about all our publications, please visit www.thamesandhudson.com. There you can subscribe to our e-newsletter, browse or download our current catalogue, and buy any titles that are in print.